# A WEEK ONE
# SUMMER

# A WEEK ONE
# SUMMER

## ASM

### FLOYD STEADMAN

First published 2021 by ASM

ISBN 978-1-8384970-8-8

Floyd Steadman would like to express his profound gratitude to Edward Griffiths, Saracens CEO, 2008-2015, for his advice and assistance in the development, writing and publishing of this autobiography.

Designed by Tim Underwood  timund@hotmail.com
Printed by Sarsen Press  www.sarsenpress.co.uk

# Dedication

At three minutes before nine on the night of 20th November 2016, my entire world came to a shuddering halt. That was the precise time when I said my final goodbye to my wife as she quietly slipped away. Denise had been fighting a short and intense battle against cancer... and everything had spiralled downwards so quickly, with only 12 weeks between the diagnosis of the cancer and her passing.

I had lost my wife and best friend, and our three boys had lost their wonderful mother, and her family – the Friggens from the village of Madron in west Cornwall – were dealt yet another blow so soon after losing Angela, an older sister, and their mother Joan.

As I said my final words to Denise, the pain and the sense of loss was almost unbearable, and I didn't know what to do next.

We had discussed so many plans, talked so happily and for so long about what we wanted to do as we grew old together.

Denise had always wanted me to write an autobiography. She knew my story and understood the challenges I had faced.

"And you should call the book 'A Week One Summer'," she added. So here it is.

This book is dedicated to the memory of Denise Steadman, my wonderful wife and an inspiration to so many people.

*Floyd Steadman, September 2021*

# Contents

# Foreword

## *Mark Evans*

I've been incredibly fortunate to have spent a good part of my personal and professional life immersed in both rugby codes – in the UK and elsewhere. This has meant I've been lucky to have met and worked with a huge number of talented, highly motivated people with great values. Amongst them all Floyd stands out.

Of course I am biased in his favour – in my twenties he was my teammate, captain and friend. We remain friends many decades later. He was a talented scrum half who went close to international honours in a crucial decision-making position that very few black English players have played in, before or since. Powerful, competitive and tactically astute he had the respect of all around him. If you were playing in the higher echelons of English rugby in the eighties, you knew Floyd.

However there was always far more to him than simply sporting prowess. He rarely mentioned the details of his upbringing in those days. Very few of us realised the barriers he had needed to overcome simply in order to play at a high level and graduate from university. We were more aware of his burgeoning career in education, his eloquence and his ability to mix so easily with people from all backgrounds. He was always so polite, thoughtful and considered that it was easy to miss his fierce determination and drive.

It was no surprise that he went on to smash through a fair few glass ceilings in his chosen field – just as he had in his chosen sport. Genuinely interested in and committed to young people, he enjoyed a stellar career as he led a variety of educational institutions, whilst at the same time building a wonderful family with his beloved wife Denise and their three sons. The way he reacted to the tragedy of her early death was quite extraordinary – dignified, measured and inspiring.

His story is fascinating on a personal and societal level. Floyd has always been proud of his heritage and fought hard to achieve at a time when racism in the UK was far more overt than it is today. He never backed down, refused to accept that he would ever be anything less than a success and continues to strive for more progress and diversity; all this at the same time as being incredibly popular and loved by those of us fortunate enough to know him well.

# Prologue
## *Maro Itoje*

Mr Steadman made an instant impression on me because he arrived as the new headmaster of our school, Salcombe Preparatory School, and he was black; he was the only black member of staff at the school and the only black headmaster that I had witnessed. As a young black boy, seeing Mr Steadman lead with such grace and authority was a great example for me to follow.

It was January 2006 and I was 11 years old. As students, we were curious about the new head and we quickly saw he had genuine charisma and a real sense of presence; he was also in great physical shape for a man in his late forties.

I clearly remember the day when he approached me while I was playing football with friends and said I should consider playing rugby union. At that time, I had no knowledge or experience of the game. He wasn't overbearing at all. He was friendly. He sowed a seed in my mind and I got involved in rugby as soon I moved to St George's School, Harpenden later that year.

We have remained in contact over the years and, as I have learned more about his experiences and achievements, I have become even more inspired and impressed.

Mr Steadman is a fantastic role model for young people, especially those who face adversity, and I am delighted his extraordinary story is now in print.

# Introduction

It was exciting and it was terrifying. A ten-year-old black boy had found the courage to escape from his abusive father and run away from home; and he roamed the streets of north London, alone, for a week one summer. It was the summer of 1969.

He felt excited because he suddenly felt free... free from the endless chores, free from the beatings, free from the bullying; but he was also terrified because he was completely and utterly alone, with nobody to talk to, with nothing to his name except the clothes he was wearing, with nowhere to live, with no hope and apparently no future.

That ten-year-old boy was me... young Floyd Steadman.

I was a youngster trying to find my place in the world, trying to blend into the landscape around me, a patchwork of sprawling looka-like suburbs: Willesden and Cricklewood, Neasden and Harlesden, Kingsbury and Colindale... bustling high streets, quieter residential avenues of mainly modest terraced housing, established white communities somehow learning to live alongside significant numbers of immigrants from Asia and the Caribbean.

For a week one summer – and then for another week, and another week – I wandered through these suburbs, trying to avoid attention or questions, each day looking for something to eat and somewhere to sleep.

The decision to run away from home was not hot-headed and emotional; it was calmly planned and had been a long time coming. My life seemed unfair. Day after day, I was given chores – clean this, clean that, scrub this, scrub that, go shopping... and no, you can't go to play with your friends.

My father was not a bad man. His life had never been easy and he worked hard to provide for me and my sister, but maybe there were times when he took his frustrations out on his son, a little boy who only wanted to impress him; and, on days when he happened to have been drinking, when he sought solace in alcohol, he would take the fan belt and beat me.

I had had enough. At the end of what would now be called Year 5, a week or so into the summer holidays, I decided to seek something better and to run away. I didn't even tell my sister Dolores. One bright July morning, I simply climbed out of my bedroom window, shinned down a drain pipe, jumped over the fence at the back of our house – and, all of a sudden, I was standing in the alleyway, alone, free, excited and terrified at the same time.

"Floyd, what are you doing?"

I gasped. It was our neighbour, a kind and friendly man. He had happened to be in his garden and had witnessed my dash for freedom. I looked at him, not knowing what to say, scared and confused.

"It's OK," he said. "Calm down. You don't have to explain anything."

He seemed to understand what was going on, and gestured towards the small garden shed at the end of his garden, opening on to the alleyway.

"Don't worry. I won't say anything to anybody but I'm going to leave the door of this shed unlocked each night, all right. You understand?"

I nodded nervously, and almost managed a thin smile as I scampered away down the alley towards the street, out into the world.

Later that night, after dark, I returned to our neighbour's shed and found he had left a blanket out for me. Such acts of kindness are not forgotten and so, for my first few nights as a runaway, I slept quite well... literally a few metres away from our house, where I suppose my father and sister were starting to wonder what was happening and where I had gone.

I was worried about being caught, and I was certainly not ready to go home, so it wasn't long before I decided it would be safer to spend the nights further away from our house. I found alternative lodging in an adventure playground in a public park in the middle of Kingsbury: there was a small, enclosed cabin at the top of the slide, and that became my bedroom.

Time started to pass more quickly. Hour followed hour, day followed day. I walked and walked, hung around the parks and often met friends from school, who seemed childishly impressed by what I had done. Fleeting moments of pride soon gave away to aching hunger. I needed to eat.

During the late 1960s, it was normal practice for many people to have milk delivered to their doorstep each morning. Whatever the weather, often before dawn, all around England, an army of 40,000 milkmen would tootle around in their milk floats – essentially carts with a dropped axle and large wheels, which created a lower centre of gravity and allowed for smoother travel over rough surfaces. They would leave one, two, three or sometimes even four pint-sized glass bottles of fresh milk for their customers, who would wake and, habitually, go to 'get the milk in' for their breakfast.

Waking early had necessarily become part of my daily routine as a runaway, and I watched the milkmen at work. I quickly recognised there would be nothing quite so easy as waiting until the float had turned the corner, quietly nipping up to a front door – any front door – stealthily taking a pint of milk, and so provide myself with a 'free' source of protein and nutrition.

Nothing would be quite so easy, and quite so wrong.

I was alone on the streets. I had no money. I had nothing to eat or drink. And yet something somewhere inside told me I would not steal. I don't know what it was. It was just a basic instinct. I was not going to steal.

Instead, I watched one particular milkman as he worked, driving his milk float, getting off to deliver the pints, getting back on to drive a little further down the street, getting off to deliver more pints, on and off.

"Excuse me, sir," I said. "Could I help you?"

"How do you mean?" he asked, looking at me suspiciously.

"Well, maybe I could work for you. You do the driving. I will run up and down to deliver the milk. We could finish the round in half the time."

"OK," he pondered, "but I won't be able to pay you much."

"Anything will do."

"Well, it will have to be 7/6d a day, not a penny more."

"That's fine," I said.

Just like that, I had got myself a job. The daily rate of seven shillings and sixpence was not much, even in the late 1960s, the equivalent of 37 pence after decimalisation in February 1971, but it was something, enough for me to feed myself and I clearly remember feeling almost jubilant.

We would typically finish the round at around nine in the morning, and then I would go to a cafe, sit alone among the working men, and buy myself a full English breakfast, which set me up for the day.

For a week one summer, I was surviving… and for another week, and another week, although I knew I had to be careful. My father would have reported me to the police as 'missing', and the constables on the beat would have been told to keep an eye out for a ten-year-old black boy.

One afternoon, while ambling along the pavement of a street in Colindale, minding my own business, I noticed a police car driving towards me on the other side of the road. I froze. I stared directly at the policeman, and the policeman stared directly at me. Eye contact prompted panic. I dived head first into a hedge beside the road, scrambled through the leaves and branches, and landed on a patch of grass on the other side. How had I done that? I had no idea, but I wasted no time in standing up and sprinting away.

Still alternately excited and terrified, I began to accept this adventure could not last forever. Eventually, after around three weeks, I decided it was time to visit one of my primary school teachers at her home and explain what had happened. She listened, and was kind and sympathetic, and she gave me something to eat.

However, she was also firm and clear that she would call the police, and ask them to take me home to my father. I didn't argue.

Thinking back now, I had unthinkingly assumed my father would be angry with me for running away, and causing him concern, but that he would still be happy to see me again and life would return to normal.

That is not what happened.

The policeman knocked, and my father opened the front door. He looked at me with an expression of complete disdain and disgust.

"I do not want him living here," he said. "Take him away."

"But, Mr Steadman," the policeman said, "this is your son."

"I said I don't want him. Take him away."

The human mind seems to have an extraordinary capacity gradually, with time, to dull the pain associated with difficult moments in life, but these words remain etched on my mind.

Aged ten, on my own, I was duly taken into care, driven away to a children's home, funded and overseen by the local council.

It was the summer of 1969... not exactly the Summer of '69 described in the lyrics written and sung by Bryan Adams. Those were not the best days of my life. But, in some ways, a line had been drawn in the sand, and a new chapter was about to begin.

# Chapter 1

# **Discarded**

My childhood is a blur, a hazy series of disconnected incidents. Yes, I clearly remember running away from home and yes, no doubt, with passing time, my mind has managed to dull the pain of difficult memories.

It is sad. It's sad that I have no recollection of my mother. It's sad that I have very few positive memories of my father. It's sad we didn't seem to celebrate, or even really recognise, birthdays or Christmas. It's sad that, no matter how hard I try, I can recall so few moments of childhood happiness.

Here are the bare bones. My mother and father separated before I was one year old, and my sister and I were taken into care. Neither of us ever saw our mother again because she seems to have been chased away by our father, who threatened her with violence if she contacted us.

When I was four, we returned home to spend six years living with our father, who worked as a motor mechanic. In 1969, when I was ten, as I have related, I ran away from home. When my father said he didn't want me back, I was taken to live in a children's home. From that day, for 51 years until his death in May 2020, I had minimal further contact with my father.

Do I blame my parents?

I certainly do not blame my mother at all. It is one of the great sorrows of my life that I never knew her, that I cannot remember her at all and that I don't know what qualities I inherited from her. What kind of person was she? What did she look like? I imagine she was kind, and maybe not particularly tall but I just don't know. All I can do is imagine.

As for my father, well, looking back, a reasonable assessment may be that he was not present when I needed him but that he was, at least partly, as much a victim of his circumstances as I was a victim of mine.

In recent years, I have wanted to find out more about my family, and have searched for information not only in the various online resources but also with the authorities in Jamaica and in Brent, north London.

I have discovered my father's name was Dudley Alphonso Steadman, and he was born on April 18, 1931 in a place called Blue Mountain valley in Jamaica, in the Caribbean. He was the third of maybe ten children... we can't be sure. His father was a gardener and his mother was a domestic servant.

Life was hard in Blue Mountain valley, situated to the north of Trinity Ville and to the west of Mullet Hall. Even the distant views of Blue Mountain, the highest mountain on the island, would barely have raised the spirits of the labourers, working in the sugar fields and living in poverty.

Dudley's spirits may well have been lifted, however, when he started dating Isolyn Thomas in 1956. He was 24, she was 16 and he had an idea. "Why don't we leave this life behind," he said, "and go to live in England?"

So, the records state, this young couple bought their tickets on a boat that set sail from Kingston on April 18, 1956 and duly arrived in Plymouth in May. One of Dudley's older brothers may have travelled with them. We can safely assume these young people emigrated to Great Britain with equal measures of excitement and apprehension about what lay ahead.

They travelled in hope... hoping to escape the poverty of their lives in Jamaica, hoping to find opportunity and a better life in England. For some immigrants from the Caribbean, such high hopes may have been fulfilled. For others, they found only a new kind of poverty and discrimination.

Literally millions of words have been written about the experience of those who emigrated from the Caribbean to Great Britain, invited to assist the rebuilding of the country after World War II. On a personal level, I can only imagine the emotions of my parents as they travelled into the unknown.

Dudley and Isolyn arranged to get married soon after they arrived, and their wedding was held at St Gabriel's church in Cricklewood on September 1, 1956. In the church register, the occupation of the groom was listed as 'motor mechanic'. Isolyn was already pregnant and, the following January, she gave birth to a daughter, named Dolores, born in Broadstairs in Kent. A son, me, arrived 20 months afterwards, born on September 4, 1958.

Nobody ever told me why my parents named me 'Floyd', but it is surely not a coincidence that Floyd Paterson was the heavyweight champion of the world on the day I was born. The American had beaten Tommy Jackson in an elimination bout on November 30, 1956, becoming, aged 21, the youngest boxer ever to win the title. There followed three epic fights against Ingemar Johansson, of Sweden, when he lost and then regained the belt, and Paterson remained heavyweight world champion until he lost to Sonny Liston in 1962. He retired in 1972 when, aged 37, he was beaten by Muhammad Ali.

I have always felt pleased to have been named after a great sportsman, who once noted: "They said I was the fighter who got knocked down the most, but I was also the fighter who got up the most." Looking back on the experiences of my childhood, I can identify with the sentiment.

Floyd Paterson also once said: "When you have millions of dollars, you also have millions of friends."

Well, in September 1958, it's accurate to state Dudley Steadman had neither millions of dollars nor millions of friends. His new life in England was turning out to be more challenging than he had hoped and now he was obliged to look after two young children, in addition to his teenage wife.

Maybe it was all too much. Their marriage took strain and, a few weeks before my first birthday, my parents decided they would get divorced. Our family unit of four was broken a few months after it had been formed.

My sister and I were led to believe my father was given custody of his children because, after the divorce, our mother had simply disappeared. That is what we were told. In fact, that is not true. We were misled.

According to the file held by the Children's Services department of the London Borough of Brent, both my father and my mother had applied for custody. An acrimonious legal contest ensued, and it was decided that Dolores and I would be taken to a state-owned residential nursery, where we would be looked after until the case was heard and finally resolved.

The file also includes papers stating my mother had wanted to visit us at the nursery. My father told her to stay away. She came anyway. He found out, and beat her up so badly that she was taken to hospital with broken bones, and he was sentenced to serve six months in prison for inflicting grievous bodily harm.

The fifth of the Ten Commandments prescribes: 'Honour your father and your mother'. It's fair to say my father did not make it easy. If his aim was to scare my mother away from her children, he succeeded, sadly.

I never saw my mother again. Isolyn Steadman, née Thomas, was born on April 24, 1940 and died in June 1994 following a heart attack. Those are the plain facts, and the plain facts are all I have. There are no papers, no photos, no memories... just a hole in my life.

In 1962, when I was four, Dolores and I were taken from the children's home and returned to live with our father in Harlesden; with hindsight, we were probably better off being looked after by paid carers rather than by a man who struggled to control both his drinking and his temper.

Random memories still lie in and around my mind, like fragments of shattered glass scattered on the floor... still capable of cutting me, and making me bleed, if I think back too much about what I have experienced.

Some memories are harmless and fine... my father regularly used to take us to visit somebody who we called 'aunt'... she lived nearby, somewhere in north London... I don't know whether we were actually related but I remember she used to feed us particularly hot curry goat, rice and peas.

Other memories are sharp... we were often cold because we had no central heating... and that meant we would try to keep warm by huddling around a basic paraffin stove... and, on one occasion, my sister sat too close to the stove and her dress caught fire... it was a terrifying moment... everybody seemed to panic... Dolores was running around the room screaming... she suffered burns, which, as I remember, needed to be treated in hospital...

Some memories are sharper still... I recall feeling as if I was always being told what to do, always being told to keep quiet... I remember being locked in my room for no apparent reason, not once or twice but regularly...

The winter of 1962-63 became known as the Big Freeze in Britain, with temperatures plummeting to levels only seen twice since records were started in 1769. Rivers and lakes froze over, sport was disrupted and, outside our home, my father's car was often snowed in... as he said, he needed to get to work so we had to dig the snow away. This chore was allocated to me, a four-year-old boy. I struggled with the spade. I hated every minute and yet, early in the morning, when required, I would get the call to dig out the car.

Unsurprisingly, subjected to such treatment, I became a nervous and anxious child, and I started wetting the bed, but there was not much sympathy. I was not allowed to change the sheets, and gradually became accustomed to falling asleep and waking up in sodden and stinking linen.

It is possible now to reflect with some kind of perspective, and even some level of understanding. But, at the time, it was difficult to exaggerate the impact on a small boy. I was made to feel utterly unloved and useless.

In the absence of any other explanation, I began to believe it was all my fault. Had my mother left us because of me? I didn't know. Did my father bully and beat me because I deserved nothing more? I didn't know.

We are all a product of experiences and, today, maybe it is easy to understand why I tend to wrap my three sons in cotton wool and why I am determined to ensure they feel loved and supported at all times... and perhaps it is also easy to understand why, during my career as a teacher and headmaster, I was so resolved to confront and eradicate any bullying.

It did not take long for my father to marry again. My sister and I soon found our lives were further complicated by the arrival of a step-mother, and then of step-brothers and step-sisters. Maybe it was inevitable that we started to feel like outsiders in our own home, essentially in the way.

Of course, life was not easy for anybody. My father worked exceptionally long hours as a car mechanic, and was often busy in evenings and weekends, and my step-mother worked hard as a nurse... maybe that explains why they felt my sister and I should do so many jobs at home. Maybe they felt the familiar brand of old-fashioned Caribbean 'tough love' discipline was the most effective way to mould us into responsible adults.

"Dad, please can I go out and play with my friends?"

"Have you completed your chores?"

"No, but..."

"Floyd, I have warned you before."

And so I grew to believe my life was unfair, and so, aged ten, I ran away from home in the summer of 1969... and so my father told the policeman he did not want me back home... and so I was taken into care.

What happened to my father? I am really not sure. He continued with his life, and I continued with mine. There was one occasion, maybe a decade after I was taken into care, before I went to college, when I needed to get a parent's signature on a grant application form. So I made contact with him, and asked for his help. He initially refused. He only had to sign. That was all. I persisted, and, at the last minute, he did agree to sign.

However, it was clear to me he had no real interest in keeping in contact. That was absolutely no problem for me.

The records say my father married again, to a woman called Pearl Broughton; they appear to have lived in Kenton and – so far as I can remember, and I may very well be mistaken – they had four children, two girls, Sharon and Jennifer, and two boys, Steve and Christopher.

I don't believe I have ever met any of these half-sisters or half-brothers, but I am not certain.

One day, many years later, maybe in the early 1980s, when I was working during the summer holidays at a shop called The Adidas Connection in Tottenham Court Road, London, somebody walked into the store out of the blue and introduced himself as Steve Steadman. He said he was my half-brother.

I have a memory of us chatting quite amicably for a while, but there was nothing more to it. There were no smart phones in those days, of course, and I suppose I wasn't really interested. Whatever the reason, we did not stay in touch.

There was another phone call, maybe in the 1990s, from somebody who said he was my uncle, one of my father's brothers. We spoke politely for a while, and we said we would meet, but we never did.

Steadman is not a particularly common name in London, but I felt no need or urge to dig up the past and make contact with anybody. As time passed, I was much more focused on building some kind of future.

The years passed until, in 2015, my wife Denise finally persuaded me to reach out and make contact with my father and my sister. She said nobody could change what had happened in the past, but she felt some form of reconciliation would help everybody, including me, finally to move on. I wasn't so sure, but Denise's judgement was usually right, so I agreed.

The first step was to locate my sister. We had not spoken since I was taken to the children's home when I was ten, but I managed to find her and it quickly became clear she had faced significant challenges in her own life and yet, to her credit, she seemed to have settled and found stability.

Dolores and I spoke at length. We discussed the past, and what had happened in the intervening years. She told me all about her five children, and I told her about my three sons. We have remained in contact ever since, either calling or texting each other every couple of months.

I told her I was thinking about making contact with our father, but she strongly felt this was not a good idea at all. My sister had continued to suffer through her teens, living with him after I left home. I don't know exactly what happened, but it was clear their relationship

9

had broken down completely, and she had not spoken to him for some time.

She did tell me she thought he had followed my career over the years, that he knew I had played rugby and become a headmaster, but she was not sure and, again, I found myself feeling detached and disinterested.

"Don't do it, Floyd," she said firmly. "Don't contact him."

Dolores' advice resonated. The principle of reconciliation is sound, but, for my father and me, too much had happened. He had walked away when I had really needed him when I was young. Yes, he was an old man in his eighties, but he was still responsible for his actions. I explained to Denise why I would not contact my father, and she understood.

Dudley Steadman died in hospital in May 2020. My sister called to tell me the news. I was sad, of course, but that was all and that was that.

Being estranged from my family meant I became somewhat removed from the Caribbean community in London. This was not a conscious decision, but there was very little Caribbean presence at my school and college. Then, there were relatively few West Indians either in and around rugby union or at the schools where I worked, and there were obviously no family gatherings.

There was, however, Roger Loubon, a barber of Caribbean descent who worked at a place called Evolution in Hanwell. I became friendly with him when I began to teach, and have visited him regularly ever since. In fact, my sons have also had their hair cut by him. I have always enjoyed sitting in the chair, listening to Roger's news and being immersed in the Caribbean patter of the customers who liked to gather and chat in his shop; over all these years, it has been a regular point of contact with the West Indian community.

That is nobody's fault. It's just the reality.

Make no mistake, I have always been proud of my roots, and would one day very much like to visit Jamaica and maybe even to walk through Blue Mountain valley and get some understanding of the world my parents left behind when they made a decision to emigrate to England in 1956.

However, the unavoidable reality is that I was abandoned by my family... and left alone... left alone to find my own way forward in life, to find any way forward after being discarded.

# Chapter 2

# Saved

There were approximately 102,000 looked-after children in the United Kingdom in 2020; that number has been increasing steadily year after year since the turn of the century. A 'looked-after child' is defined as a child who has been in the care of their local authority for longer than 24 hours, living either in a residential home or, more often, with foster parents.

Well, there is no doubt that I met the official criteria and could certainly be described as a looked-after child because I was placed under the care of the London Borough of Brent not for 'longer than 24 hours' but for seven years, from the age of ten until the year before I left school.

The term seems to carry connotations. When you tell somebody you were a looked-after child, they tend to assume that life in care must have been grim, that conditions were appalling, that you were physically and sexually abused by secretive monsters on a regular basis.

That was not my experience... not at all.

Let me introduce you to Aunt Betty and Uncle Bill, two of the most kind and most decent people you could ever wish to meet.

It sounds ridiculous but I actually don't remember their surname... and I also don't know how I will ever be able to thank them properly for what they did for me when I was discarded and most in need. The chaos and cruelty of life at home was replaced by calm and kindness.

"Hello, Betty, let me introduce you to Floyd," said the council officer.

"Hello, Floyd," she said, smiling broadly and warmly. "Come in. Let me show you to your room and get you something to eat."

Bill and Betty were 'house parents', paid by the council to look after nine boys in a large Edwardian home in north London, on the border between Willesden Green and Cricklewood. I remember there were three rooms for the boys: one single, a triple and a dormitory for five. As the youngest boy in the house, I was ushered to one of the beds in the larger room.

The other boys looked at me cautiously, assessing the new arrival. I looked at them with equal uncertainty. This was my new world and it quickly became clear I would have to work out my place in the hierarchy, and make sure I got along OK with the older boys. Looking back, the basic human survival instinct is extraordinary, even among the very young.

The route from the doorstep rejection by my father to acceptance by Uncle Bill and Aunt Betty was not direct. On that day in 1969, the policeman had taken me to a large residential home on Barretts Green Road, Willesden, behind the Central Middlesex hospital. This place could be described as a holding pen for children taken into care, usually because they had been abused or neglected, sometimes because their families just could not cope.

According to the way the care system worked at the time, I would stay at this large residential home, with around 30 other children in a similar situation, until the local authority could find me a permanent place in a smaller children's home. In my case, this process took around four months.

Yes, of course, it was strange to be taken away suddenly from my father and sister, even as they continued with their lives barely five miles away… but, no, it was actually not too bad. The people looking after us were gentle and kind, and I felt safe. The bed wetting stopped almost immediately.

At Barretts Green Road, we were divided into classes and taught core subjects every morning, and we were offered various extra-curricular activities every afternoon. I recall trips to an ice-skating rink, and I remember celebrating Guy Fawkes Night on November 5th for the first time, with each of us being handed sparklers while we stood around a bonfire. All this was fun. Without being too melodramatic, 'fun' was a new experience for me.

It was early December when I was eventually taken from Barretts Green Road, and passed over to my house parents, Uncle Bill and Aunt Betty, at their home at 8 St Gabriel's Road. The address is etched on my mind. Their welcome was warm, and another new experience lay in store for me barely a few weeks later – celebrating a traditional Christmas at home.

After all the turmoil, I settled into a steady routine… waking up each morning in a loving home, going to school at Oliver Goldsmith Primary and returning each afternoon to the same loving home, where my house parents, and two other women, one living on-site and one living nearby, looked after nine boys, ranging in age from me, as an 11-year-old, to a 16-year-old.

We may not have been a conventional family, but we were a family; and I felt extraordinarily fortunate to have landed in this particular place, to be provided with food and shelter and, above all, to feel loved.

It was not a holiday camp. Certain standards were set, and we were expected to keep our rooms tidy, and to have proper table manners, and to walk with our house parents to church each Sunday, but routine and discipline never felt like an imposition to me. On the contrary, after so much turmoil, I relished the stability of knowing what was expected of me. Even at a very young age, I learned the important difference between discipline that is harsh and unfair, and discipline that is kind, reassuring and structured.

I realise others were not so fortunate, of course, and I completely empathise with the trauma suffered by some children in care, but I must say that, in my personal experience, the 'system' worked well. The council paid a reasonable sum of money to honest, hard-working people, so they would be able to look after vulnerable children who had nowhere else to go.

This payment included a monthly allowance for clothes. I recall the unbridled exhilaration of going shopping with Uncle Bill. There was also enough money for us to be taken on a summer holiday each year; we used to travel by coach and spend two weeks at a Butlin's camp by the seaside.

Butlin's was a peculiarly British phenomenon, a series of friendly family holiday camps where everything was included in the price and where activities for all ages were arranged from dawn to dusk, all presided over by the famous 'red coats' who smiled and organised with relentless enthusiasm. One year, on holiday at Butlin's in

Great Yarmouth, Norfolk, I remember being persuaded to enter a 'Mr Muscles' contest, a series of tests of strength involving exercises, weights and a punch bag. Well, I entered. I tried my best... and I won. For what seemed the first time in my life, I won.

Back home at 8 St Gabriel's Road, we were invited to join the scouts. I became a member of the 25th Willesden Scout group, and loved the meetings every Friday evening, undertaking all the activities and collecting the badges. It felt so good to be achieving something as part of an organisation, even if the walk home sometimes presented its own challenges.

Certain parts of Willesden would probably have been described as 'rough' during the 1970s, and a young black boy in full scout uniform walking home around 10 o'clock at night might well have attracted unwelcome attention. I remember being chased by skinheads a few times, but I always managed to scamper away and, after a while, the walk home felt like part of the adventure. The need to be aware, to stay a step ahead was just a fact of life.

Week by week, in their quintessentially English calm and understated manner, Uncle Bill and Aunt Betty instilled in me traits and qualities that would serve me well later in the life. They taught me the value of doing things properly, of generally staying on the straight and narrow and resisting the temptation to seek short cuts. They encouraged me to try my best in every situation, and just to try my best. There was no point complaining about factors I could not control. It would always be enough to try my best.

Aunt Betty would be outraged by any suggestion that she had any favourites among the boys living in her house, but, deep down, I do think she saw something in me. She pushed me harder than the others, often insisting that I stay home to finish my homework when the others were allowed to go outside and play, as if she somehow expected more of me.

It was not long before she moved me out of the large dormitory for five and into the single room, usually reserved for a much older boy. Rightly or wrongly, I felt she was looking out for me, and that felt good.

As the years passed, boys came and went, arriving and leaving the large house at 8 St Gabriel's Road. Maybe that explains why I have no clear memory of any of them. Strangely, frustratingly, I am unable to recall any names or faces of my housemates. I have searched my memory, and come up with nothing.

There is one name I do remember... Dennis Nilsen.

We often used to play football in the garden and, unavoidably, now and then, somebody would kick the ball over the fence into a neighbouring property, and one of us would have to walk around and retrieve the ball. That was no problem, except I remember there was one adjoining garden where none of us would go. I don't recall any specific discussion about why we would not go into this particular garden. It would have been late 1975 and early 1976, and each of us understood we would not go to this place. We accepted that, if the ball did go there, we would leave it. No argument.

The 'forbidden' garden belonged to a ground floor flat at 195 Melrose Avenue, which – it transpired – in 1975 became home to Dennis Nilsen, a 30-year-old Scot, and his 20-year-old friend, David Gallichan.

Nilsen became notorious as the serial killer who murdered at least 12 young men and boys in north London between 1978 and 1983, eight of whom were lured to this same address in Melrose Avenue by the promise of food and alcohol, and then strangled. The bodies were first stored beneath the floorboards, and then cut up and burned on a bonfire... while, perhaps 30 yards away, Uncle Bill and Aunt Betty ran their home.

In general, it was agreed boys would leave 8 St Gabriel's Road at the age of 16, after completing their CSEs or O levels. I asked to stay longer, because I wanted to remain at school and study for A levels, qualifications required for me to become a PE teacher.

Uncle Bill initially thought this would not be possible but, after some debate, a compromise was reached with the local authority whereby I would stay for an extra year in St Gabriel's Road, and would then move out in August 1976 and rent a room in the home of one of my teachers.

So, I duly left the home of my house parents as an increasingly self-assured 17-year-old, a far cry from the anxious eleven-year-old who had arrived in December 1969. Then, almost unbelievably, I lost contact with Uncle Bill and Aunt Betty. That's the way things were done. That's how the system worked. I moved on. Other boys moved in. That was that.

I did write a few letters in the weeks that followed, letting them know how things were going in my last year at school, but communication soon ebbed away and it was only via the grapevine that I heard, maybe three years later, that Uncle Bill had passed away. Aunt Betty, somebody said, had decided to move and live somewhere on the south coast.

Around ten years later, in 1986, in my mid-twenties and newly married, I felt the urge to contact Aunt Betty because I wanted to introduce my wife, Denise, to the person who had effectively been my mother through my teenage years, who had, in so many ways, saved me.

I made a few telephone calls, and managed to track her down, and called her and arranged for Denise and I to visit her home. It was a happy and emotional meeting. I think I wanted her to see that I was OK, that I was doing well and that I had found a wonderful woman to be my wife. That was the last time we spoke. I don't know why. That's just how it was.

What would have happened to me if I had not been passed into the care of Uncle Bill and Aunt Betty? I shudder to think, and I realise I owe to this couple a debt I will never be able to repay.

Stability and routine at home had been complemented by stability and routine at school. In 1970, I managed to pass the 11-plus exam and duly progressed from Oliver Goldsmith Primary School to Kingsbury High School. I was excited, ambitious and determined to be the best I could be... and then frustrated when it seemed I was being held back in lower forms because black children were perceived as less academic than white children.

That's a contentious claim, I know. It's how I felt at the time.

"Floyd, you should plan to do something with your hands," they told me. "Some kind of vocational training would be ideal for you."

"No," I would reply. "I want to be a teacher and, if I want to become a teacher, I need to take A levels. That's what I want to do."

"Yes, something with your hands would make sense."

"No, I want to be a teacher."

The same conversations were repeated over and over again.

I don't doubt these teachers meant well. I am not suggesting they were either overtly racist or malicious, but they do appear to have demonstrated at least some degree of unconscious bias in their assessment of my potential… in their blinkered eyes, as a looked-after black boy, I was not able to take A levels and secure the qualifications required to become a teacher.

My response was to persist, and persist, and persist. There were no arguments or hysterics. I wanted to take A levels, because that is what I needed to be a teacher. In my view, education was the key to my future. In my opinion, it was an education which would open doors to a better life.

Kingsbury High School was a giant school, the result of a merger between Kingsbury County Grammar and Tyler's Croft Secondary Modern School when the London Borough of Brent adopted the comprehensive system in 1967. There were no fewer than 300 children in each year group, and each year group was split into 12 streams, ranging from the brightest downwards.

So Class 1A included all the brightest students, and Class 1L included the pupils who were often referred to as 'ESN', educationally sub-normal. It's sobering to remember how children were classified scarcely a generation ago. Only the top five classes – 1A, 1B, 1C, 1D and IE – would take O levels.

That was the bare minimum for me. Being placed anywhere below 1E would be a disaster, and effectively condemn me to the shadows.

I vividly remember the day of decision, the first day of term, when the list of classes was posted on the notice board, and I stood among an anxious group of students, straining to learn our fate, excitedly scanning the lists to find my name.

Class 1A… nothing.

Class 1B... a couple of my white friends from primary school, none of whom had done better than me in class, but not me.

Class 1C... no Steadman there.

Class 1D... more of my friends from Oliver Goldsmith, but not me.

Class 1E... third from last, Floyd Steadman, listed just after Yioda Panayiotou, a friend who had a brother called George, who would later became famous as the celebrated singer/song-writer George Michael.

Yioda and I had just scraped in to the lowest O level class, even though I had performed well at primary school. This did not seem fair. I looked again at the lists. There were no black students in 1A, 1B or 1C. How was this possible? There was no answer but again there were also no arguments or hysterics. Just work hard, Floyd, I told myself, control what you can control.

It didn't matter if the most motivated and talented teachers were allocated to 1A and 1B. It didn't matter if the general levels of application and motivation were much higher in 1A and 1B. It didn't matter if, for all these reasons, it felt so much harder to get decent grades in 1D and 1E than it was in 1A or 1B. I could not control such decisions. I could only control how hard I worked, how hard I tried to overcome the unhelpful circumstances.

So I applied myself and secured seven O levels, four Bs and three Cs; these grades earned me the right to stay at school and take two A levels, in Art and Geography. I had hoped to study A level Chemistry as well, because, odd as it may seem, I enjoyed playing with acid and creating explosions. However, the Chemistry teacher told me this would not be possible because he did not trust me. I was disappointed at the time but, looking back, with the benefit of hindsight, his judgement was maybe not an example of unconscious bias; it was, in truth, an example of common sense.

It was no problem. I set myself the target of gaining two A levels, which would be sufficient to secure entry to a teacher training college.

At Kingsbury High School, in class and beyond, I started to make real friends, proper friends who I liked and who liked me, friends who I could rely on. At the age of 12, this was another brand new experience.

"Hi, my name is Des Benjamin."

"It's good to meet you. I'm Floyd Steadman."

And so a young Jewish boy became friends with a young black boy at high school. More than 40 years on, we are still friends.

There were others in our circle: with Des, there was Ian Franks, Eric Atkins, Richard Crowther, Nigel Flynn, Glen Smith, Malcolm Crisp, Mick Robinson, Kevin Childs and Neville Brown. We played sport. We fooled around. We were normal teenagers.

Why did I make friends at school, and not in the children's home or even at 8 St Gabriel's Road? I am not sure. Maybe, in care, your primary concern is survival and, in survival mode, you are reluctant to be too open, to give too much of yourself and make friends. Perhaps, in school, among others of your own age, among others with similar tastes, habits and ambitions, it is easier to give and take, to share things and to get along.

Des and I certainly got along. His family lived in an apartment in Pinner and, most Saturday evenings, after sport, I would go around to the Benjamins' place, and his mother would cook us food. Often I would stay the night, sleeping on a mattress and we would wake on the Sunday morning, and his mother would have prepared a full English breakfast, a real treat.

He lives in the country these days, but Des and I still meet up now and then, and remember the old times. We met for a meal in London some time ago, and my friend seemed agitated.

"Floyd, there is something I need to tell you," he said after a while. "It's been on my mind for many years, and it's annoying me."

"OK," I said, now intrigued, wondering what was coming next.

"Well," he said, "you remember all the times you came round to our place."

"Of course, I do. Your family were always very kind to me."

"Yes, well, it was around that time that my parents suggested we should ask you to move in and live with us permanently. We all thought of you as one of the family, and they said it would be a logical step."

"OK."

"But I said no. I said I wanted you to be my friend. I didn't want you to be living with my family. So my parents dropped the idea. I am sorry. I was so selfish. I was only thinking of myself."

Initially taken aback by this revelation, I paused for a moment and then told Des not to worry. "I appreciate you telling me," I said, "but don't feel bad. If I look back on my life, it is the tough times that have made me stronger, that have made me the person who I am. Those were difficult years for me, but I had to fight for myself and that did me no harm."

If I had been in his position, I would have reacted in exactly the same way.

Sport was always important at Kingsbury High School, and I enjoyed regular opportunities to play football, cricket, basketball, badminton, squash, athletics, cross-country running… everything except swimming; – ever since being dunked by some older boys, I have steered clear of the pool.

However, my life changed on the rugby field.

Brian Jones, a PE teacher, a Welshman, was speaking. "Right, you lot," he shouted, making himself heard above around 150 11-year-old boys, all waiting for instructions. "Every Saturday morning, you'll play either football or rugby. You can't play both… it's either or."

He proceeded to approach the boys one by one and declare either 'rugby' or 'football'. It was his call, a simple selection process. Boys who were told they would play rugby walked across to the rugby fields, and boys told they would play football headed for the football pitch.

Mr Jones looked at me… maybe a little small for my age, maybe a bit broader and stronger than most. "You will play rugby," he declared. And so I did… for the next 20 years, rugby would be a central part of my life.

My first ever training session followed. I remember feeling as though I was the smallest player on the field. We played a match, 15 against 15, even though I had no idea what I was doing. Nobody in my family had ever played rugby. In fact, nobody in my family had ever shown so much as a passing interest in rugby. And yet I enjoyed myself. I enjoyed the feeling of the ball in my hand, enjoyed the physicality, enjoyed the challenge to be brave and courageous. I even started to enjoy the spirit of the game.

At one stage, a much taller, stronger boy was running towards me, straight at me. There was no escape. Unaware of any skill or technique, I basically threw myself at him, grabbed something, held on and somehow managed to pull him to the ground. I had executed what was the first tackle of my life. I could get to like this game, I thought. I could like it a lot.

The impact of an enthusiastic teacher is extraordinary. Mr Jones enjoyed rugby, and he was able to transfer this love of the game to so many of the youngsters who happened to be standing on those school fields.

The impact of being told you are doing well is extraordinary. When Mr Jones saw me somehow tackle the larger boy, he shouted: "Yes, Steadman, that's the way." And, almost instantly, I felt happy and enthusiastic about the game, about me as a person, about life, about the world.

A positive experience on the rugby field followed upon a positive experience on the rugby field, and I began to change as a person, gaining confidence, gaining self-belief, at last gaining some degree of self-esteem.

In my first year, I played for my House in an Inter-House tournament at school, with each team including boys from across three year groups. I was one of the smallest boys on the field, but I loved every minute and ran around, manically tackling anything that moved. And our House won the competition, and I was called up to the stage at what seemed a vast school assembly, and was presented with the trophy in front of the entire school.

"Wow, look at Steadman," one boy said.

"Apparently, he's really good at rugby," said another.

In my second year, our Kingsbury High School team managed to win the major Middlesex Under-14 knock-out tournament involving 40 schools from around the county. Other schools such as Bishop

Douglass, William Ellis and Chiswick were strong, but we emerged victorious, winning the final played at what was then the Wasps home ground, in Repton Avenue, Sudbury.

It is no exaggeration to say I found myself on the rugby field. I found a role, a significance, a purpose and a level of self-confidence which had seemed unimaginable before I started playing the game.

When a boy teased me during a French lesson, I thumped him. When another boy made an insulting remark about 'Love Thy Neighbour', a popular television comedy show about a working class white couple living next door to a more educated black couple, I told him to meet me in the playground after school; a group of boys gathered, chanting 'fight, fight, fight', and I piled into him, and only stopped when I was literally pulled away.

Please understand, I am not advocating fighting. It was dumb. However, it is probably true to say that Steadman the slightly timid looked-after child was almost overnight transformed into Steadman the combative rugby player, and the two were almost unrecognisable from each other.

I had started as a hooker because I was small and physical, had then been moved to number eight at the back of the scrum because I loved tackling, and eventually found my place at scrum half, where I could be a physical presence both in defence and in attack.

Success followed success. As an under-15 school team, we beat several major independent schools, won the County sevens tournament, the County 15-a-side competition and played the entire season without losing a single match. Our unbeaten team included no fewer than seven boys of colour, which was remarkable when you consider there were only around ten boys of colour in our entire year group of 300 students… only ten in the year, and seven of those ten were in the rugby first XV. In any case, we barely noticed the racial break-down. We loved the game. The irrepressible Mr Jones was always there, always supporting; and we kept winning.

"Floyd, I am putting you forward for county trials," he told me one day.

"Thank you, sir."

As I gained self-respect, so I gained muscle, especially around my neck and shoulders. I was becoming a useful rugby player realising his potential in a useful school rugby team, coached by Brian Jones; and I began to thrive for not only the Kingsbury High School, but also for the Middlesex Under-16 squad and even for the London Division age-group side.

"Floyd, I want you to captain the team this season," Mr Jones said.

I was surprised. Everybody thought the captain was chosen from the boys in their last year at school, but this was my penultimate year. Mr Jones backed me again, and I remember feeling so proud to be captain of the school rugby team for my last two years at Kingsbury High. In the second year, I was also named as captain of the Middlesex county schools side.

"Floyd, what do you think I should do here?"

Other boys were asking my advice. That was a first.

Success on the rugby field was not quite matched by success in the class room but I managed to secure the two A levels.

During my last year at high school, after leaving 8 St Gabriel's Road a year after I was supposed to move out, I was able to rent a room in the home of Mr Jones and his family, a neat semi-detached home in Woodcock Hill, Kenton, north London. There were two children, a daughter Ann, two years older than me and a son David, who was a year younger. They accepted me without a blink. Their kindness was boundless. I will always be grateful.

Was everything perfect? No. Nothing is ever perfect.

There were inevitably times when I did feel like an intruder in the Jones home, as if I was somehow invading their family space. Now and then, it would have been natural for them to feel this way.

There were also times when, despite success on the rugby field, I wondered whether I was denied opportunities because of the colour of my skin – at Kingsbury High School, the head boy and deputy head boy were elected by the pupils and staff, and many said they intended to vote for me.

Nigel Flynn was clearly, and deservedly, destined to be elected as Head Boy, but people were saying I had performed well as a school prefect and had a strong chance of being elected as his Deputy. However, when the results were announced, a white boy was named as Deputy Head Boy. I was disappointed. There was no evidence the process was fixed. I am just relating how I felt at the time.

Don't worry, Floyd, I told myself. As usual, control what you can control; there were no hysterics and no arguments. I had long since accepted that hardship and adversity were facts of my life, and I had long since resolved to respond by being persistent, by working hard, by doing things properly as Uncle Bill and Aunt Betty had taught me... and, increasingly, by demonstrating the quiet self-confidence instilled in me by Mr Jones.

Brian Jones continued to teach at Kingsbury High School after I left, and he died in 2006. There were many, many mourners at his funeral, though I doubt whether any had as much reason to thank him as me.

Looking back, I was incredibly fortunate to find Uncle Bill and Aunt Betty as house parents at 8 St Gabriel's Road, and I was doubly fortunate to find Brian Jones as my rugby coach. In my view, the combination of these three people effectively saved me, effectively saved my life.

I might so easily have drifted in the wrong direction, succumbed to the easy temptations of crime, anger and blaming everybody else. Instead, these three people – three decent, hard-working people – provided me with guidance and love, and kept me moving in the correct direction.

In the years that followed, working as a teacher and then as a headmaster, I would sometimes hear particular children being described as a 'wrong'un' either because they did not quite fit or because they behaved badly. As a result, too often, they would stray and underachieve, and find themselves living without hope on the fringes of society.

I would wonder what was the difference between me and a 'wrong'un'? How close did I come to being blankly categorised as a 'wrong'un', condemned to a life where I had no opportunity to realise my potential.

Maybe the difference was very small.

Maybe the difference was simply love and guidance. I was shown love and provided with guidance at important moments during my formative years. It would become the overriding ambition of my adult life to do to others as had been done to me.

So the looked-after black boy left school and headed to college. In so many ways, he had effectively been saved.

# Chapter 3

# Inspired

The Northern Irish accent was broad but clear. "We need a decent scrum half, so we're making you an unconditional offer," said John Hunter, first XV coach at Borough Road College.

It frankly didn't seem to matter whether I was a looked-after child or the heir to a titled member of the aristocracy. It didn't seem to matter whether the colour of my skin was white, black, yellow or green. They needed a decent scrum half, and they had decided that was going to be me.

Not for the first time, nor the last time, rugby opened doors for me. The game was my passport to a better life.

I was determined to become a teacher, and had fought for the right to take A levels and gain the necessary qualifications to gain entry to a teacher training course; and I was also eager to attend one of those colleges which focused on sport, because that seemed to be where my talent lay. On the sports field, more than anywhere else, I felt equal to everyone else.

There were a few options. Loughborough University was well known and highly respected, and there was St Luke's in Exeter, Jordanhill in Glasgow, Carnegie in Leeds, St Paul's in Cheltenham,

Cardiff Training College and Borough Road College in Osterley, west London. They were all just names to me but, in the end, after a fair amount of asking around, I submitted applications to St Paul's and Borough Road College.

"Candidates must have played at least two sports at county level."

The requirement was clear, but that was OK. I had played rugby for Middlesex, and I had also been included in the county squash squad. For good measure, I added I had been invited to county cricket trials. The process was daunting. I suppose, deep down, I doubted whether I would ever have the opportunity to go to college. Wasn't that something that happened to other people? I didn't know. I simply didn't know, but I completed the application forms and posted them to the addresses provided, and hoped for the best.

Both St Paul's and Borough Road responded, and invited me to selection days, which I duly attended, always doing my best and working hard to look as if I belonged in such elevated, elite environments. In the end, St Paul's made me an offer conditional on decent A level results and – via John Hunter's telephone call – Borough Road College made me an unconditional offer.

BRC needed a decent scrum half, and so my future was decided.

I was excited, and even a bit stunned. Borough Road College was founded by Joseph Lancaster in 1798. The oldest teacher training college in the entire Commonwealth, it was renowned for the excellence of its sport and physical education, and I had been offered an unconditional place.

Years later, Clive Woodward would say he thought every aspiring young rugby player should try to attend a specialist sports college. England's Rugby World Cup-winning coach felt such institutions offered both the time and also the facilities for young players to develop, essentially to do everything that young professionals would be able to do in years to come. This was my experience. BRC was an ideal place for me, and for my rugby.

There was, however, one last hurdle to clear. The college said it was necessary for my father to sign the application form for the bursary. I made contact with him for the first time in years, and asked for his help. He refused. I asked him again, explaining I didn't need any money or support from him… all I needed was his signature on the form. He refused again.

"Can't you just manage without my father's signature," I asked somebody at the college. "We haven't spoken for the last nine years."

"I'm sorry, but those are the rules," came the reply.

I clearly remember one dismal and desperate moment when it seemed certain that my dreams of going to college would be shattered just because by father refused to sign this piece of paper. I asked again. I begged. And, at almost the last possible moment, Dudley Steadman signed on the dotted line. I recall that I thanked him, and never, ever spoke to him again.

Brian Jones shared my relief and excitement, and helped me prepare for the challenge that lay ahead.

"You need to make sure you are ready for Borough Road," he told me. "It will be a step up from anything you have known so far, and you'll be competing with some of the best young players in the country."

"So what I should I do," I asked.

"You need to train at the club throughout the summer," he said. "You need to be fitter than ever by the time you arrive at college."

When Brian said 'the club', he meant Wasps. During the previous season, midway through what was my last year at school, he had told me the west London club were starting a schoolboy team, and they wanted me not only to play scrum half but also to captain the side. It had been a great experience, and I enjoyed feeling part of something.

The Wasps schoolboy team had done quite well and, towards the end of the season, I was asked to play a couple of games for the Wasps second XV. People started to talk about me. People started to notice me.

"Well played, Floyd," said Blackie, "that's the way!"

That was the Geordie accent of Alan Black, captain of the Wasps seconds, a legendary figure at the club and one of the great characters of the game who would go on to work for many years at the Rugby Football Union. He seemed to see something in me, and was always encouraging. It's hard to exaggerate the impact of a kind word from somebody you respect.

So I trained at the club's ground in Sudbury throughout that summer, often on my own, getting fitter and stronger than ever. I took part in the Wasps trials at the start of the season, and was made to look good by a talented young fly half from Waterloo, named Ian Ball, who caught every pass I threw at him.

"Steadman looks sharp," someone would say during training, and, day by day, I started to feel myself becoming more confident and self-assured. When it was time to go to college, I was flying.

The big day eventually arrived. I packed two bags, left my room in the Jones family home and took a bus to the Halls of Residence.

Those two bags contained absolutely everything I owned in the world: some clothing and a few personal belongings. For me, there was no bedroom back at the family home. There was no home and there was effectively no family. I was on my own, carrying a duffel bag and a battered suitcase.

It's strange how some memories stick in your mind. As I walked through the gates of the Halls of Residence, where I had been allocated a room, I recall seeing another student arriving by car with his parents, driving right up to the front door. I stood quietly in the shadows, and watched as his obviously proud father helped him carry a trunk and several suitcases to his room.

Oh well, I thought, that's his world. I am living in a different world. There is no point complaining, or feeling sorry for myself, or becoming bitter. I decided to keep my head down and meet every challenge, to work hard and do my best, without arguments or hysterics. That was my way.

This difficult moment of feeling alone and inferior quickly passed, as it almost always did, and, later that evening, when the parents had left for home, I felt more calm and comfortable. Whatever our backgrounds, wherever we came from, we were all essentially in exactly the same boat – new students in new surroundings, all hoping to make friends and settle quickly.

"Hi, my name is Floyd," I would say, "do you play rugby?"

Nobody needed to know my story. Nobody needed to know the reality of my situation. It would not define me.

As I recall, out of around 120 students starting their first year on the physical education course, there were three black youngsters – a basketball player, an athlete and me. We became friends and we settled quickly, eager to make the most of the opportunity presented to us. In those days, no more than seven percent of school leavers went to higher education.

Were we aware of being regarded as different? Yes. Was some level of racism accepted as being normal in the late 1970s? Yes.

"Come on, Floyd, it's your turn now. What are you going to sing?"

Borough Road College rugby club, like almost every other rugby club in the world, and indeed like the England international squad, had its own initiation ceremony, where new players were formally welcomed after playing their first match. These rituals invariably took place in the bar and usually involved plenty of alcohol, singing and good-natured humiliation.

"Come on, Floyd, what song are you going to choose?"

I was poorly prepared, and hesitated.

"No problem, we can choose a song for you," somebody said. "Come on, boys, let's help Floyd with a song. You all know the words."

So they started to sing, and urged me to sing along with them... and, to my eternal regret, I did sing along with them. I wanted to fit in. I wanted to feel accepted. I wanted people to like me.

And so I sang...

*Sambo was a lazy coon,*
*Who liked to sleep in the afternoon,*
*So tired was he, so tired was he.*
*Off to the forest he would go,*
*Swinging his chopper to and fro,*
*When along came a bee, a bloody great bumble bee,*
*Bzz, bzz, bzz, bzz.*

And so they sang – and so I sang – this awful racist song, which seemed to be quite well known to many people at the time. There is no doubt that, if asked to look back and reflect on these events, my former teammates would say they meant no offence and that it was just a bit of fun.

I believe them. It was a different age. What is viewed as completely unacceptable now was widely regarded as normal and unremarkable in the late 1970s. The 'Black and White Minstrel Show' was one of the most popular shows on BBC television for 20 years, with white performers blackening their faces and singing a variety of western songs and folk ballads. Many people spread Robertson's marmalade on their toast at breakfast, unconcerned by the fact that the branding on the jar featured a golliwog.

It would be as nonsensical to look back and suggest every member of the BRC rugby club was a racist as it would be to say everyone who watched the Black and White Minstrels or enjoyed Robertson's marmalade was a racist. It was a different age, with different standards of behaviour.

All that said, even now, I find it hard to forgive myself for joining in the song. I was new to the college and I did want to be liked and accepted, and indeed I wanted to be picked in the first team, but I wish I had not been so easily swept along.

The words still grate...

*Sambo was a lazy coon.*

It was not until at least five or six months had passed, until I felt more confident within the environment, until I was prepared to make a stand, until I finally found the resilience and courage to say no.

"Come on, Floyd," they urged. "Sing your song."

"No."

"Come on, be a good sport, sing your song."

"No, I'm not going to sing that song."

It's accurate to say I felt substantially more comfortable and self-assured on the field. The competition for places was intense. In both my first and second years at Borough Road College, I was in and out of the first team, but I was generally happy and enthused, relishing every moment in an elite environment.

Towards the end of my first year, I was included in the Borough College team at the annual Middlesex Sevens at Twickenham. It was a major event on the rugby calendar in those days, and it was incredible for me, as an 19-year-old, to have the opportunity to run out in front of a crowd of 50,000 people and to play at one of the great rugby stadiums in the world.

Rugby was giving me unimaginable experiences in unimaginable places, and I was thriving. We generally played twice a week, once against another college or university team on a Wednesday and then again on a Saturday, against a senior club team. I looked forward to the weekend matches because we were a team of super-fit students and, more often than not, we would run our older opponents off the park in the second half.

I was constantly improving. My box kick off my right foot was reasonable, the result of countless sessions with Brian Jones, where he would tell me to stand outside the 22m line and kick into the five-metre channel. My right-hand pass was decent but, if I'm honest, I needed to work on my left-hand pass. In time, I developed a long, accurate dive pass, which meant I could get the ball away from traffic and give possession to our backs in space.

My strengths were firstly communication – I was always talking, bossing the pack around, telling the forwards what to do and where to go – and secondly power and speed in the red zone, inside the opposition 22m line. That was my territory. Sensing any kind of gap around a set piece, or a ruck or a maul, I would back myself to break a tackle or two and burst clear. The fliers on the wing were certainly faster than me over longer distances, but there were not many players who could catch me over 20 metres.

I had scored 61 tries in 60 matches in my last season at Kingsbury High School and, when I started to replicate this kind of form at Borough Road, people took notice and it was not long before other opportunities were presented.

Augustus Beverley Walter Risman was a legendary figure at the college, where he was employed as a lecturer. Bev, as everybody knew him, had been one of a select group of dual code internationals, having represented England first in rugby union and then in rugby league. He played fly half for England in eight matches between 1959 and 1961, and also played four matches for the British and Irish Lions on tour to Australia and New Zealand in 1959. He then switched to play rugby league for Leigh in 1960, and played five times for Great Britain before completing his career with five seasons at Leeds.

As a notorious 'defector' to professional rugby league, Risman was effectively banned from playing any role in what was still amateur rugby union, but he slipped through a loophole because he was employed as a lecturer at Borough Road, and so he was permitted to succeed John Hunter as first team coach for what was my third year at the college.

We got along well. I admired him in every way, and he seemed to appreciate my enthusiasm and approach to the game. He was well connected in rugby, and was instrumental in me being selected to play for the British Colleges side, and also for England students. These are just words on a page, which can easily be glossed over, but, at the time, playing for each of these representative teams felt like a massive achievement.

I continued to play scrum half for the first XV in my third and final year at Borough Road College, and enjoyed a season notable for victory over our rival, Loughborough University at our home ground in Isleworth. There was no grandstand and only a few hundred supporters, but it felt like a big day for us.

Rugby was creating so many opportunities for me... opportunities to be good at something, opportunities to feel good about myself, opportunities to meet new people and, in those days, opportunities to travel. Touring has always been one of the greatest features of the game; strangely, and sadly, there seem to have been more rugby tours in the 1970s and 1980s than there are today.

At the end of my first year at college, I was selected in the Middlesex Colts squad to tour Portugal; that was my first ever rugby trip abroad and a fantastic week ended with a win over the Portuguese Under-20 team. At the end of my second year, I was named in the Borough Road College squad to tour Northern Ireland, a trip organised by John Hunter at the height of the troubles... "whatever you do, don't talk about politics," I remember being told.

By normal standards, such trips may seem unremarkable. For me, following a childhood in care, such trips felt like nothing less than a magic carpet ride. To repeat, rugby was giving me unimaginable experiences in unimaginable places, and I felt so fortunate to be so immersed in the game.

If the term times at Borough Road were wonderful, the three annual holidays proved more challenging. Where would I go? What would I do? I had ceased to be the responsibility of the local authority's care system on the day of my 16th birthday. So, as soon as term ended, I was on my own.

For the Christmas holidays from mid-December to mid-January, for the Easter holidays from mid-March until mid-April and then for the summer holidays, for three endless months from early July until early October, I needed to make my own arrangements, to find somewhere to live, to find some kind of work to pay my rent and living costs, somehow to survive and get by.

Each holiday presented a new set of circumstances, and needed a new plan. On one occasion, I found a cleaning job at the West Middlesex hospital, which paid enough for me to rent a room nearby. Another time, I worked in a meat processing factory in East London. Another time, I managed to find employment as a tennis coach. Another time, the Vice-Chancellor of Borough Road College, one of the very few people aware of my predicament, discretely arranged for me to keep a room in the college Hall of Residence.

The combination of such acts of kindness and my developing survival instinct generally kept me out of trouble, and enabled me to get through the holidays and turn up for the following term, ready to study and play again.

I used to worry about Christmas, and dreaded spending the special day on my own. That never happened. To my great relief, each year while at college, one of my friends invited me to spend the day with them. In those three years, I spent the first Christmas in London, the second Christmas in Bury, Lancashire, and the third Christmas in Blaina, in the South Wales valleys. I seriously did not want to be alone. So many people were so kind.

Was I angry or bitter? I really wasn't. I accepted the challenge of each holiday as my reality, and set myself to find a solution. Becoming angry or bitter would not have helped in any way. As ever, without hysterics and without argument, I simply put my head down, worked hard and found a way.

"Hey Floyd, do you fancy joining me at training with London Welsh?"

The question was being asked by Gareth James, partner of Gwen, one of the PE teachers at Kingsbury High School. It was Gareth who had been kind enough to invite me to spend Christmas with his family in Blaina. Thoughtful and supportive, he became one of my closest friends, almost like an older brother to me, one of the few people on whom I felt I could completely rely. He was also an outstanding rugby player, with fantastic hands, and he was keen for us to train together during the holidays.

Well, I thought, it would make a change from going down to Wasps, so I turned up at Old Deer Park with Gareth and found myself training with the likes of JPR Williams, Mervyn Davies, John Dawes, John Taylor and Gerald Davies, icons of Welsh rugby.

Looking back, my life was extraordinary. I was working in a meat processing factory during the day, earning pennies to get by, and, that same evening, I would be training alongside genuine legends of the game. I used to watch them carefully, studying everything they did, imitating and learning.

I eventually left Borough Road College, after three years, with the qualifications I needed and a few great friends.

Andy Phillips was also a member of the rugby team. He was a tall and strong winger from the Midlands, and he would eventually be best man at my wedding. Steve French was another teammate, who would emigrate to live near Perth in Australia. Paul Cochrane was a talented rugby player and also a fine cricketer – he used to take me along to play for the North Mimms Cricket Club in the highly competitive Hertfordshire league.

These friends, and others, supported and encouraged me, and helped me get through the difficult moments, to such an extent that I now reflect on my three years at Borough Road as being among the happiest of life.

Yes, there were hardships. Yes, there were moments, particularly during the holidays, when I didn't know how I would survive, but, in the words of William Butler Yeats, I was indeed fortunate to have such friends.

Others were not so lucky.

I had a friend at college. His Christian name was Derek. I don't remember his surname, unfortunately. We met each other by chance, and we seemed to get along well from the start. It wasn't long before we realised that we had a great deal in common. He was also a looked-after child. He had overcome significant adversity to secure his place at Borough Road College.

While I was primarily a rugby player, Derek was a talented gymnast, so we often trained in different places and at different times, but we generally made sure we met for a coffee, or a beer, three or four times each week. I used to enjoy chatting to him because we seemed to be on the same wavelength. He appeared to understand me, and I understood him.

We were friends throughout the three years at college, and we finished at the same time, ready to move on to the next stage of our lives. At least, that's what I thought would happen. In fact, just a few months after leaving Borough Road, Derek threw himself off the cliffs at Beachy Head, near Eastbourne, and committed suicide. I guess he simply felt overwhelmed.

News of Derek's death left me feeling shocked and devastated. He had fought so hard in difficult circumstances and had achieved so much but, I supposed, he had reached the conclusion that everything was too much. I didn't know. He had never spoken to me about thoughts of taking his own life, and I wondered whether there was anything I could have or should have done to help. Maybe I might have been more available to meet and talk with him.

The thought also crossed my mind that – in other circumstances – it could so easily have been me who, in that moment of desperation, felt so hopeless that there seemed no good reason to carry on struggling and living.

Thinking back, I am convinced that what made the difference for me was the kind intervention of key people at key times... of Uncle Bill and Aunt Betty who took me in to their home at 8 St Gabriel's Road... of Brian Jones who gave me the chance to play rugby... of John Hunter, who offered me the opportunity at Borough Road... of Bev Risman, who saw my potential in the game and helped me earn selection for a series of representative student teams... and of Gareth James, who so often took me under his wing.

I was fortunate to benefit from the kindness and support of all these people, and of my friends.

Derek, sadly, was not so fortunate, not so inspired.

# Chapter 4

# Accepted

So far as I could see, I needed to choose where I was going to play my rugby and there were three potential clubs in London.

Would it be Harlequins, the most prestigious of the three? Would it be Wasps, where I had trained and played as a youngster? Or would it be the quirky and in some ways unfashionable club in north London, Saracens?

Thankfully, as my studies at Borough Road College drew to a close, all three clubs let me know they would be keen to secure my services, which left me with what felt like an important decision to make.

Harlequins were the blue bloods, the rugby club of choice for top players from the top universities, such as Oxford and Cambridge, gliding along a gilded path towards top jobs in the City of London. For a certain breed of aspiring young rugby player, Quins was the only choice. For me, even if I was swiftly growing in self-confidence, particularly on the rugby field, I was not so sure whether I would be able to thrive at such elevated levels.

Rugby was still firmly established as an amateur game, and clubs were obliged to be creative as they lured players to join their ranks.

Quins relayed the message to me that, if I did decide to make my way to The Stoop, their home ground in the lap of Twickenham, I would be most welcome to join the club tour at the end of the season, at no cost to me. I thanked them for the offer, and said I would let them know in due course.

Wasps was a club built around some wonderful characters like Alan Black, an upbeat and influential presence, and Sir Peter Yarrington, a lovely man who was President of the club and later President of the RFU. I obviously knew my way around the ground at Sudbury from my experiences in the youth teams, and the west London club was strong and ambitious; the first team was packed with players apparently destined to play for England.

I wondered whether they were perhaps too strong. Would I ever get a game in the star-studded first team at Wasps?

Saracens offered more certainty, in happily familiar tones. The Northern Irish accent was still broad and it was still clear.

"We need another scrum half," said John Hunter, the selfsame coach who had given me the opportunity at Borough Road College and who was now coaching the first team at Saracens. "Come and join us, Floyd," he said.

There were other options in and around London. The three Exiles clubs, London Irish, London Welsh and London Scottish, all had their own appeal and identity, and the likes of Richmond, Rosslyn Park and Blackheath always attracted their fair share of players. But, in my mind, the decision came down to one question: where was I going to play the most first team rugby?

For the second time in my career, John Hunter had provided the answer, so I agreed to join Saracens for the 1980/81 season and

Sadly very few photographs of my childhood remain, except these pictures of me with Kerry, grand-daughter of Uncle Bill and Aunt Betty, *above left*, and, *above right*, Christmas 1978 with my close friend Gareth James, his wife Gwen and his mother. *Below*, the Kingsbury High School under-15 team was unbeaten, with me third from right in the front row, one of seven black players in the side.

Brian Jones, physical education teacher at Kingsbury High School, inspired me to play rugby and gave me confidence; he is shown here with his daughter Ann, *above left*, wearing his Middlesex Rugby blazer, *above right*, and, *below*, in his element, giving instructions on the rugby field.

*Above*, the Old Kingsburians team won a Sevens tournament in 1978 and, *below*, getting the ball away under pressure from Bedford during the early years at Saracens, with Ian Peck, my opposite number, on the left. *Overleaf,* in action for Saracens in a Middlesex Cup match against Ealing.

We may have been amateurs but we played hard, on and off the pitch, and I eagerly embraced a fancy dress party at London Welsh, *above*, and, *below*, post-match celebrations with my Saracens teammates following delivery of a welcome plastic yellow watering can full of beer.

*Above left*, taking a pass from Alex Keay and, *above right*, attending a Saracens dinner with John Buckton: both remain great friends. *Below*, we were presented with a Rugby World 'Team of the Month' award during 1988/89. *Overleaf*, playing against Pontypool RFC in the snow at Bramley Road.

headed to Bramley Road, the club's warm and rickety home ground in Southgate.

Saracens rugby club was formed in 1876 by old boys of the Philological School in Marylebone Road, subsequently known as Marylebone Grammar School, and their first matches were played on the fields at the back of Primrose Hill, to the north of Regent's Park. A nomadic existence followed, through no fewer than nine home grounds, before the club settled into a permanent home at Bramley Road immediately after the end of World War II in 1945.

If Harlequins were the blue bloods, then maybe Saracens was a place where blue collar workers felt more at ease. Whatever it may have lacked in pedigree, 'Sarries' stood on its own in north London – in contrast to the plethora of established clubs virtually falling over one another to the west and south of the city. The club was able to recruit talent from a relatively vast area stretching across Hertfordshire to the north and Essex to the east... in years to come, a young Ben Clarke would arrive from Bishop's Stortford, and a prop by the name of Jason Leonard would make his way from Barking.

I arrived at Bramley Road and quickly felt at home, at training on Tuesday and Thursday evenings, and on match days sometimes in midweek and always on Saturdays. What about the gym sessions, you may ask. This was 1980, a time when, even at leading clubs, rugby players rarely found their way to the gym. The pre-match meal was a full English breakfast, and we could scarcely spell the word 'nutrition', let alone appreciate it's value.

As it turned out, Saracens endured a relatively disastrous season in 1980/81. John Hunter left the club before Christmas after a series of disagreements with the captain, and we lost no fewer than 34 of our 46 matches, including record defeats against Moseley, Coventry and Rosslyn Park.

"The only way is up," somebody said. They weren't joking.

On a personal level, I was satisfied with my performances. A houseman doctor named Chris Milford was the incumbent scrum half, and his work commitments meant he was only available to play every other weekend. It worked out that we effectively shared the first team No.9 jersey, with him playing one week and me playing the next, an arrangement which gave me time and space to settle into the club and start to make my mark.

Somebody was kind enough to remark that the emergence of me and a gifted winger named Pat Kamara provided at least two reasons to be hopeful at the end of what was otherwise a poor and dispiriting campaign.

We struggled. Stephen Booty was a fine hooker, but he left to join Wasps at the end of the season. Kevin Douglas was an outstanding open side flanker, who would excel for several seasons before leaving the club to devote more time to his career as a teacher at an independent school.

Such was the nature of club rugby in the 1980s. Almost everybody had to work to earn a living. Unavoidably, people came and people left.

Many of the old stereotypes applied. The forwards were typically big, hard men, often policemen or labourers, who relished the physical elements of the game, while the backs tended to be bankers or PE teachers. On long coach journeys to away matches, the backline players looked forward to getting stuck into The Times crossword while the forwards played card games and gambled.

We did salvage some pride with a decent run in the Middlesex Cup, defeating Wasps in the semi-final before losing to the Metropolitan Police in the final, but all the chat around the clubhouse was that results were not good enough, and that changes would be made to improve the situation.

I was only 23 years old, more accustomed to listening than talking but, within six months, I was appointed as club captain.

This unexpected sequence of events began when a new broom swept through the club after the poor results in 1980/81. Roy Fawden was elected as President, Barney Richards as the secretary and Chris Sneath as the treasurer, and a sense of renewal was sustained by the appointment of Andy Harrower, a 23-year-old centre, as the youngest club captain in 40 years.

Andy worked as a teacher and he appeared to be the future but, just before Christmas 1981, he opted to switch careers and take a job in the Metropolitan Police. The rules at the time stated that anyone who was fully employed by the Met was obliged to play for the Met, so he had to leave Saracens in the middle of the season, creating an immediate vacancy as captain.

Maybe some people were surprised by my appointment. There was plenty of coverage and comment in the newspapers, and it was certainly unusual for an established English club to appoint a black man as club captain, but I was oblivious to such considerations. The decision did not come as a surprise to me. I was established as the first team scrum half, and I had begun to find my voice on and off the field, organising, encouraging, being involved, making suggestions. I do not want to sound arrogant, and I was genuinely thrilled and humbled, but I was not at all daunted by the responsibility. On the contrary, I was excited by the challenge of leadership. I knew I could do the job.

Maybe my experiences, often facing adversity from a young age, had made me more sanguine than most, rarely indulging in extreme emotions, preferring to accept and assess every situation, to develop a plan and then to execute that plan calmly, always avoiding arguments and hysterics.

I had captained the Kingsbury High School team in my last two years at school, and enjoyed every aspect of the challenge: motivating each player as individuals and encouraging the squad as a group, sitting with the coach and expressing my personal opinions on team selection, representing the club in the correct manner way before, during and after each and every match.

All this was known and understood. What I had perhaps not appreciated was the time commitment required of the captain.

I was working as a physical education teacher at Edgware School, and my life became a frenetic blur.

Over and above each weekday as a full working day at school, plus taking sport on some Saturday mornings, and my own training to stay physically fit... there was usually a selection meeting on Monday evening, two hours of squad training on the Tuesday evening, a midweek match against a college or touring team on the Wednesday, the second training session of the week on the Thursday evening, a rest on the Friday and the match on the Saturday, with coach trips to and from away games every other week.

The workload was demanding, but I was not complaining. I loved the routine. I loved working hard and being ridiculously busy, I loved the collective sense of achievement when things went well. I even loved the challenge of trying to find an effective solution when something went wrong.

Saturdays were rarely dull. I would often have to referee a schools match starting at 10:00 and then, straight after the final whistle, rush to my car and drive to reach an agreed place at an agreed time, where I would park the car and jump aboard the Saracens team coach en route to wherever we were playing, somewhere like Bath or Gloucester... and then I would play the full match and be captain, and get home in the small hours.

I wasn't complaining. That's just how it was. I didn't know anything different.

"How many matches did you used to play each season," one of my sons asked me not long ago, expecting me to say around 30, which is what a regular club player would expect to play in, say, 2020/21.

"It was usually around 60 games per season," I replied.

His mouth dropped open.

I continued: "Yes, it would have been around 60. That would be around 40 first team matches for Saracens, plus five or six county matches for Middlesex, and a few divisional matches for London and then there would be the odd invitation match for Public School Wanderers, and an end-of-season tour. In total, there were generally two matches each and every week."

"OK," he said, "but I suppose the rugby wasn't as physical in those days."

"You're right," I said. "Most of the players in the 1980s would look quite feeble compared to the body-builder physiques of modern rugby players, and there is absolutely no comparison between the relatively gentle impact of the collisions in our day and the bone-shuddering hits of today. The game was certainly not as physical back then... but it was unquestionably more brutal."

"More brutal? What do you mean?"

"Well, the modern game has rightly been cleaned up, with cameras tracking every move and ensuring every offender is cited and punished. In our day, the referee tried to keep control as best he could but, in reality, when the referee happened to be looking the other way, a player could get away with just about anything. The result was an extraordinary level of brutality."

"Like what?"

"Like having an opposing player gouge your eye with his fingers; and like being punched either at the bottom of a ruck, or in a scrum or even out in the open. Such assaults were relatively common and widely accepted as part and parcel of the game. More extreme violence, like having your testicles squeezed in the clenched fist of an opponent, was more rare, but you would expect to receive such treatment, on average, once or twice per season."

"OK, too much info, Dad."

"Well, you asked."

"That must have been horrible. Why would you put up with that?"

"The brutality was part of the game. It was how we played and, invariably, whatever happened on the field was forgotten over a few beers in the bar after the match. That was our kind of rugby. And I loved it."

I soon learned to look after myself. If an opposing player ever took a cheap shot at me, unseen at the bottom of a ruck, I understood what needed to be done and actually became quite skilled in the art of 'accidentally' elbowing an opponent in the ribs and saying "oh, I am sorry, I didn't see you there", just to let them know they shouldn't take any chances.

Somehow, I managed to avoid any serious injury, with one exception.

It would have been in 1983 that I took a knock during training and started to experience some discomfort in my groin. After several days, the discomfort became pain. It will pass, I thought, so I continued to train and even played a match on the next Saturday. I remember it was an away game at Newbridge RFC in Caerphilly, South Wales. As the match wore on, the pain in my groin became what I can only describe as extreme agony.

OK, I thought, this is not going away, so it's perhaps time to see the doctor, who happened to be on duty at the game. He took a quick look, and said I should see a friend of his, a doctor who specialised in that region of the body and who, luckily, also happened to be at the game.

A brief inspection produced a diagnosis of testicular torsion, which occurs when a testicle rotates, twisting the cord that carries blood to the scrotum. The abrupt reduction in blood flow is what causes the agony. The doctor told me I should go to hospital as soon as I got back to London.

So I did exactly as I was told and was immediately admitted to hospital, and sent for emergency surgery to remove one of my testicles. This procedure eased the agony, but I was kept in a ward for two weeks, under supervision, until the doctors were satisfied there was no infection, and even then I was not allowed to return to rugby for another month. I have to say just recalling these events is a profoundly unpleasant experience.

The first team showed signs of improvement in the 1981/82 season, and the general club morale was lifted by six wins against strong opponents, including a surprising victory over Coventry in our last match.

I can still remember the roar of relief from the crowd of almost 1,500 when the final whistle was blown at Bramley Road. The Rugby Football Union had chosen 22 clubs to form something called the Senior Clubs Association, and Saracens was maybe slightly fortunate to be included in this elite. It had become clear that results needed to improve if we were to maintain this status, and the win over a strong Coventry side, which included Peter Rossborough, the former England full back, kept the critics at bay for another year.

The structure of English club rugby was slowly evolving from the traditional series of 'friendlies' between long-standing rivals, but it would be five seasons before leagues were launched.

I was happy. We seemed to be moving in the right direction. Alex Keay had been appointed as vice-captain and, together, we set about creating a strong, supportive and positive culture which was felt not only in the first XV but in all the teams which the club fielded each weekend... the second team was called the Crusaders, the third team were the Infidels, the fourths were known as the Turks, the fifths as the Griffons, the sixths as the Saladins, the sevenths as the Scimitars and, last but not least, there were the Colts.

The club invariably fielded no fewer than eight teams every weekend. It was a substantial organisation, driven by volunteers content to give to rugby so much more than they would ever expect to take; as a young black man, I felt hugely proud to serve as the club captain of this great club.

In years to come, between 2011 and 2019, a golden era when the club was winning multiple Premiership and European titles, it would frustrate me when unaware journalists would write about Saracens as if they were some kind of artificial All-Star team, recruited out of thin air by a wealthy benefactor. That was not the case. The origins of that all-conquering team, captained by Brad Barritt and led by Nigel Wray, were firmly rooted in many decades of history

Simply playing for Saracens, let alone captaining the team, would have been enough to keep me more than busy but, in the early 1980s, ambitious young players were expected to make themselves available for their club, and also their county, and also their divisional side as well. These were the tiers of the rugby pyramid, with the England team at the top.

I had been selected to play for Middlesex teams all the way from schools and youth teams to the county team, and enjoyed playing with the three seaxes emblem on my jersey. It has always felt good when, in an article or merely in conversation, somebody refers to me as a 'Middlesex man'.

Within the established system, players who excelled at County level tended to be invited to London Division trials, and the divisional team would be selected to play against the South West, the Midlands and the North.

As time passed, it gradually dawned on me that the various selection panels deemed me good enough to play for Middlesex, and often to captain the side, but rarely good enough to play for the London Division.

I was frequently left feeling highly frustrated. Why was I being overlooked by the divisional selectors? Was it because I was black?

There was no evidence to suggest this was a factor. Perhaps it was because I played for Saracens rather than the city-slicker clubs like Harlequins and Wasps.

There seemed no logical reason for my regular omission, and rumour poured into the vacuum. I tried not to get involved, preferred to keep my head down and, as they say, let my rugby do the talking on the field.

It appeared I might get a chance one year when Steve Bates, the first choice scrum half, was injured and the Daily Express speculated on who might replace him in the London Division team: "Saracens' Floyd Steadman heads the list of candidates," ran the report, "and he is expected to withstand competition from Richmond's John Cullen and Blackheath's Tristan Reed."

The team was announced... and I missed out again.

Happily, I was required more frequently by the selectors of the Public School Wanderers, an invitation rugby team similar to the Barbarians which played an interesting combination of regional fixtures and celebration games, and every now and then undertook a tour to a developing country.

The club was formed in 1940 by Charles Burton, a journalist, with the aim of providing cricket and rugby to public school boys in their holidays; it became 'open' after World War II, with players only being invited to be a 'Wanderer' if they were considered to be 'a credit to their sport' and committed to 'entering into the spirit of maintaining the high standards of play and conduct achieved by generations of preceding club members'.

I appreciated the ethos of the club, and thoroughly enjoyed their approach to the game; it was typical Barbarian rugby, constantly throwing the ball around, playing with freedom and smiles on our faces, and then, without fail, sharing a drink or three with our opponents in the bar afterwards.

This was rugby union in its purest form. I mentioned previously that an established club like Saracens was only able to field eight sides every Saturday because so many volunteers in so many roles were prepared to put so much more than they could ever hope to take out. What was their motivation? Well, I choose to believe they loved the ethos of rugby, and were willing to contribute simply because they wanted the game to thrive and wanted others to have the opportunity to enjoy everything the game had to offer.

Public School Wanderers provided me with many wonderful memories, not least when we played against a New Zealand Combined Services team at the Wasps ground on Wednesday 4 December, 1985. It was the only time in my career when I lined up with my teammates before kick-off and faced the *haka*, the Maori war dance made famous by the All Blacks.

Wayne 'Buck' Shelford captained the touring team that day; little did we know he would return to coach Saracens in 2002.

So this was the landscape of my life by the end of the 1981/82 season: I was teaching at Edgware School, captaining and playing for Saracens, Middlesex and the Public School Wanderers, and, every now and then, getting a run off the bench for the London Division. I was busy, happy and totally immersed in the game which I had genuinely grown to love.

Above all, at last, I felt settled. Best of all, I felt accepted.

# Chapter 5

# Respected

In 1982, the well-respected Coventry coach participated in a coaching seminar organised by the Rugby Football Union and declared: "English rugby will never progress until we get rid of Mickey Mouse sides like Saracens."

He was entitled to his opinion, of course. As a club, our collective task was to prove him wrong, to show we could contribute to the game, to demonstrate at the very least that we deserved to be respected.

We succeeded.

In the 1988/89 season, we won all our league matches before Christmas and maintained an unbeaten record at home as we won the Second Division of the national leagues, securing promotion to the First Division. In seven seasons, the Mickey Mouse club had effectively been transformed and was established as a worthy member of the English club rugby elite.

The story of this seven-year revival merits a book on its own. I was present from start to finish, attending almost every training session, playing in almost every match. Together with so many officials, coaches and players, we gave up so much time, made so many sacrifices, and strained to win and improve our standing in the evolving merit tables and leagues.

Why?

Not for the money – we were not paid.

Not for the glory – our promotion to the First Division in April 1989 was not celebrated with a triumphant ticker tape parade through the streets of north London, with a million ecstatic supporters lining the pavements to salute their heroes waving from the top of an open double-decker bus.

So many of us committed so much to the process because we loved the game, because we loved the club and because we loved each other. Just like so many others at tens of thousands of rugby clubs around the world, we wanted to feel a sense of belonging to something, a sense of striving for a common goal and, if things went well, a sense of shared achievement.

I certainly do not include myself among those who regard rugby as somehow more noble than other sports, as somehow superior, as somehow a class apart, and I completely understand the same ethos and sentiments can very often be experienced by teams in football, cricket and many other sports.

However, for what it's worth, in my experience, in my life, there have been few greater pleasures than the extreme sense of satisfaction that I felt when sitting on a wooden bench in a changing room after a hard game of rugby, feeling a little battered and bruised, aching and maybe even bleeding... surrounded by my teammates, many of whom were close friends and all of whom were feeling just as exhausted and just as happy that they had faced the challenge together and fought together and, now and then, won together.

Anybody who has sat in such a changing room, amid the sweat, the worn kit scattered on the floor and steam billowing from the hot post-match showers, maybe with a beer in hand, will understand what I mean.

They will understand why so many of us were so motivated to give so much time to our game, to our club, to each other, just to sit on a wooden bench in a changing room after a hard game, together.

The seven-year Saracens surge, between 1982 and 1989, may indeed merit a book on its own, but one of the greatest stories ever told – the parable of the Good Samaritan – requires just 161 words in the Gospel according to St Luke, so I will try to be succinct in relating what took place.

The 1982/83 season started with an embarrassing defeat to Old Gaytonians, a junior club team, but we recovered to produce our best start in six years. Andy Phillips, my friend from Borough Road College, had joined the club and finished as our leading try-scorer with 14 tries. No fewer than 15 players had appeared in more than 22 matches, and consistency of selection was thus established as the foundation stone of our improvement and success.

I stood down as club captain at the end of that season, after deciding it was necessary to devote more of my time to being a teacher and a husband, and was succeeded by Alex Keay, a great man and a great player. He oversaw an improvement in the quality of our forward play in 1983/84, and we recorded four wins in our Merit table matches against London clubs, including a notable first victory away at London Irish in more than a decade.

Tony Russ had arrived, from Eastern Counties, in February 1984 and became first team coach. He was knowledgable, thoughtful and highly committed, and his appointment quickly accelerated our development.

We continued to make progress in 1984/85 and were not once but twice presented with a bottle of champagne, the prize given to the Daily Telegraph team of the week. We earned this accolade by winning away at Bridgend, and then again by securing a victory at Gosforth, in Newcastle.

Our backline was strengthened by the arrivals of John Buckton, a talented centre from Hull, and Laurence Smith, a 17-stone giant wing/centre who had been playing for Tabard in Radlett, and we scored a total of 92 tries, more than a 50% improvement on the previous season.

Of no lesser significance, Arthur Smith finally announced his retirement as the club's touch judge. In those days, each club was expected to provide someone to run the line and assist the referee and Arthur, one of the most lovely people I have ever met, was the Saracens touch judge for 26 years. I remember how, after the end of his final match, he was presented with a silver plate by Peter Wheeler of Leicester, the England hooker at the time.

National Merit tables were introduced for the 1985/86 season and, even if few people fully understood what seemed an overly complex system, the proven combination of Tony Russ as coach and Alex Keay as captain guided us to no fewer than 28 victories in the Second Division. We would actually have been promoted if we had defeated Orrell in our last league match, but we lost and so needed to be content with third place, a decent effort.

Once again, the quality of our squad was improved by the recruitment of two outstanding forwards, Lee Adamson from Wasps and

Raza Khalili, who came from Swansea University. Coaching, culture and tactics are always important, but it is extraordinary how often people can overlook the simple reality that top class players often combine to make a top class team.

Alex Keay had said he was going to retire at the end of 1985/86 but, happily, he was persuaded to stay for one more season, a fourth successive campaign as captain. Again stability would prove important, but we were inconsistent in 1986/87, losing to Old Reigatians, Reigate Grammar School Old Boys, in the John Player Cup, then beating Blackheath and Rosslyn Park in the league.

After playing around 450 matches for the club, Alex was finally allowed to retire and leave to start his coaching career at Blackheath. Lee Adamson was appointed as the new captain and hopes were raised by the return of Andy Phillips after a spell at the Metropolitan Police, and the clever recruitment of John McFarland, an Ulsterman and a hooker who would become an outstanding coach with the Bulls, the Springboks and the Sharks in South Africa, and the arrival of a tough loose forward by the name of Dean Ryan, who would also develop into one of the most admired coaches in the game.

We were confident. We even had a sponsor on our jerseys for the first time, with the logo of brewers Greene King emblazoned across our chests, and we probably should have won promotion but fell narrowly short, finishing third in the second division, just behind Liverpool St Helens.

After all the near misses, the 1988/89 season was earmarked as the campaign when we would finally win promotion into the First Division of what were then known as the Courage leagues. I agreed to return as club captain and the vice captain was Sean Robinson, the older brother of Andy who would play for Bath, England, and later coach both England and Scotland. In so many ways, rugby used to and still does resemble a small village where almost everyone seems to know almost everyone else, which probably explains why the game seems to have so many rumours and so few secrets.

Our team was bolstered when a promising young England schools prop called Jason Leonard arrived from Barking. He would stay for only two seasons, unfortunately, before moving across London to join Harlequins and, by then, he had made the first of his record-breaking 114 appearances for England.

We started the season strongly and survived a bizarre scare when a Middlesex RFU committee cited an ancient bylaw and threatened to close down the club, actually force us to close the doors, because more than five Saracens players had been sent off the field during a two-year window. We appealed to the RFU and, following a tense hearing, common sense prevailed.

As a sport, rugby has always seemed to have a particular capacity to produce extraordinary interventions by men in blazers.

A jubilant victory over London Scottish at Bramley Road confirmed promotion, and completed for the 'Mickey Mouse' club a story which would surely have been worthy of animation by Walt Disney. Maybe that's what the Coventry coach had meant when he made his infamous remark in 1982.

Those are the bare bones of our progress, told in 999 words, a few more than the Good Samaritan. Many of the memories of these cherished rugby years are blurred, but some remain clear and vivid. I was not the type who kept detailed scrapbooks, carefully recording everything that happened.

Instead, I used to buy two or three newspapers on a Sunday morning so I could read the reports of the matches played the previous day, and, now and then, I would cut out the articles and throw them into a box alongside some of the match programmes and other bits and pieces.

Now, around forty years later, I will sometimes browse through this treasure chest, and remember many of those people I played with at Saracens, many of those people who selflessly ran the club so we could enjoy the game, many of those people and clubs who we played against. It is not a perfect system and, in advance, I apologise for any and all omissions.

I am looking through team photos from the 1980s, rows of players wearing the black jerseys with the crescent and star logo...

John Buckton stands out. 'Bucko' was a brilliant centre, as quick over 30 metres as somebody like Rory Underwood. He brought real energy to our backline, and has been a great friend to me all these years. He invited me to be best man at his wedding, and we still see a lot of each other.

Chris Babayode also played regularly in the centre, which meant there always seemed to be two or three black players in the team. He was Head of Sales at Thames Television and United Artists Programming at the time, and has had a highly successful career in marketing and media. We shared so much.

There was one memorable player fines meeting, held around the time of the race riots in Brixton, south London, when Chris and I were both found guilty of failing to participate in the riots because we were on a rugby tour with Saracens, It was just fun. No malice was intended. We didn't take offence.

Steve Hancock was a gifted Welshman who had been at Kingsbury High School with me, and he made a difference at full back for a couple of seasons. John Howe was 6'8" tall and weighed 18 stone, a wonderful lock forward who would have been a superstar in the modern game. Some years later, in 1992, tragically, John died on the rugby field after suffering a heart attack while playing for West Hartlepool at Northampton.

There was Raza Khalili, an excellent loose forward. People said his father had something to do with the Shah of Iran, and the entire family moved to the UK after the revolution in 1979. He was brilliant for us before moving to the USA, where he continued to play at a decent level.

Sean Robinson was another fine player and a good friend. I remember one evening when some of the players went to an Indian restaurant in Cockfosters after Sean had kicked the penalty to win a match. Sean brought his brother Andy, who started throwing plates around. I played reasonable cricket at the time, and managed to catch one of these flying plates. Andy wasn't too happy about this for some reason, and he and I started scuffling. Fortunately, at that precise moment, my wife and his sister-in-law both arrived and told us to stop behaving like small boys. We did as we were told.

Such boisterous, often drunken dinners were one form of what could be loosely described as team bonding, and Alex Keay and I also introduced to our training sessions the kind of chanting in unison that is more usually associated with US soldiers. We were not exactly extras from Private Benjamin, the box office hit comedy starring Goldie Hawn released in 1980, but something roughly similar took place on Tuesday evenings at Bramley Road.

As Alex and I led the players through their exercise drills, he and I would start what became known as our club chant, and soon everybody would join in...

*I don't know but I have heard it told*
*Saracens wings are made of gold.*
*I don't know but I've heard it said*
*Wasps wings are made of lead.*
*One, two, three, four... etc.*

Our most punishing training sessions took place during pre-season at Trent Park, a mile and a half from Bramley Road, the other side of Cockfosters tube station. There was a steep hill in the middle of the park, close to a monument. Coach Tony Russ would split us into pairs, and one would have to carry the other up the hill on his back, and then the pair would switch. Everybody used to try and avoid being paired with 17-stone Laurence Smith.

These sessions were exhausting and, at the end, we would be told to warm down with a gentle jog back to the clubhouse. Some bright spark like hooker Steve Jones would say, "Come on, let's race back," and some idiot like me or Grant Mansfield would accept the challenge and, all of a sudden, a group of rugby players would be sprinting through the streets of Southgate. That's just how we were... an eager, highly competitive group of friends.

We were not afraid to be different and, in fact, towards the end of the 1980s, we became the first English rugby club to introduce a qualified psychologist. Her name was Alma Thomas, and she would work with players to help them think more positively. She was talented and highly effective and, looking back, a pioneer in her field who deserves recognition.

So many remarkable people contributed so much to the club, freely giving their time to serve on the committees, attending meetings, making everything work, effectively creating opportunities for players like me to enjoy the game. Did we express our appreciation as often as we should have done? No. Did we perhaps take these men in blazers for granted? Almost certainly, yes.

Their names will forever echo through the history of the club: Bruce Miller, Bryan Smith, Chris Sneath, George Sherriff, Roy Fawden, Bruce Claridge, John Heggadon, Barney Richards, James Wyness and, doubtless, others... all wonderful men who gave so much and expected so little in return.

Of course, Saracens was only ever half of the story. In every match, in every contest, there was always the opposition... another rugby club with its own players, coaches and officials, all just as proud of their history, just as excited about the future and just as determined to win as we were.

Leicester stood apart. Mighty Leicester were the biggest club in England with the biggest crowds and the biggest stadium. In all my years of playing against them, I never finished on the winning side... not once. There was an aura about them, which started with the letters, instead of numbers, on the back of their jerseys; the front row were always A, B and C.

Players such as Dusty Hare, Paul Dodge, Rory Underwood, Les Cusworth, Dean Richards, John Wells, Tim Buttimore (who would be Jonny Wilkinson's agent), Harry Roberts (a great character from Zimbabwe) and Nick Youngs (father of Leicester and England players

Ben and Tom), were all formidable opponents, every one of them Leicester through and through.

Northampton Saints were and are another powerful club in the Midlands, and you would always expect a wonderful atmosphere at Franklin's Gardens. They drew substantial crowds and I loved playing there. Moseley, Coventry and even Nuneaton were also strong opponents in that part of the world.

We played Bedford on a regular basis, and it was never easy to leave work in London on a Friday evening, battle through the traffic on the M1 and arrive in time to be changed, warmed up and ready for a 19:30 kick-off at Goldington Road. Never easy? Actually, it was often a nightmare.

I always looked forward to playing at Kingsholm, where Gloucester would typically field a hard, strong pack of forwards, including the likes of Steve Mills, Mike Teague, Peter Scrivener, Phil Blakeway, John Fidler and others. We would always pick our strongest team to play away to 'Glaws', and we would usually lose.

Bath were one of the leading teams at the time, and it was always a pleasure to play at the 'Rec', and we would sometimes travel further to the south-west, undertaking a kind of mini-tour with a match against Exeter on the Saturday and a game with Sidmouth on the Sunday. Through the 1980s, it was really not unusual to play two matches on the same weekend.

The London clubs were our most familiar opponents.

Harlequins often produced exceptional backs, such as Marcus Rose, Jamie Salmon and Rupert Moon, a scrum half who always used to cause me problems in our many contests. They also had Dave Cook, an outstanding flanker, who was playing for Quins one

Saturday morning on the day of an international across the road at Twickenham; he was pulled off at half-time and told to get ready for his England debut just a few hours later.

Andy Harriman was another legendary Quin, a brilliant player with so much pace. We used to call him 'The Prince' because we thought he came from a wealthy Nigerian family. He studied at Cambridge University, and apparently used to drive around the town in a high-powered Porsche.

Wasps were never, ever less than difficult opponents, with players like Huw Davies, Roger Peller, Steve Pilgrim, Rob Andrew, Steve Bates, Mark Rigby (who would later become President of the club) and, of course, Rob Lozowski (whose son Alex would later play for Saracens).

Side by side in south-west London, Rosslyn Park and Richmond were strong clubs with distinguished histories. The 'Park' team often included Andy Ripley, a magnificent player and one of the great characters in the game. 'Rippers' and I played many times in the same Middlesex team, and it was much more fun to play with him than against him. Meanwhile, at the Athletic Ground, Richmond maintained high standards, and scrum half Mickey Connor was always a skilful, talented opposite number for me.

Beyond these English clubs, Saracens maintained an admirable tradition of making time each season to play the leading clubs in Wales, for some reason with the exception of Cardiff. We grew accustomed to travelling by coach to the Principality season after season, playing against these proud clubs, almost always it seemed, in cold and wet conditions, and usually we would be physically dominated and soundly beaten.

It was authentic, hard rugby and, personally, I loved every minute. We would literally be kicked around the park by Abertillery RFC, at the top of the Ebbw Fach valley in Monmouthshire. We would be knocked around by Neath RFC at the Gnoll, would be pulverised by Pontypridd RFC at Sardis Road, would be battered by Bridgend RFC at Brewery Field, and be pounded by Pontypool RFC at their home ground, Pontypool Park.

Now and then, I must admit, we would be left with the distinct impression that the players and officials of the Welsh teams enjoyed nothing quite so much as an opportunity to impose themselves on the smart 'softies' who had travelled down from London.

From our perspective, our progress between 1982 and 1989 was perhaps most accurately measured by improved performances in Wales. I remember a great win over Bridgend and a famous victory over Newbridge. It felt very good to go to places where we had usually been overwhelmed, and to win.

Rugby used to take us further than Wales and, through the 1980s, I was very fortunate to travel the world on rugby tours variously organised by Saracens, by Middlesex RFU and by Public School Wanderers.

Players would sometimes be expected to raise sponsorship money to cover costs – and, on these occasions, I was invariably supported by club officials at Saracens – but, more often than not, we were not required to pay anything at all.

Touring was regarded as our perk. Touring was generally understood to be the most welcome fringe benefit of the amateur game.

We would travel as a group, we would relish every moment on and off the field, and we would return home with wonderful memories. It is hard to exaggerate quite how much I enjoyed these trips.

My first senior tour was in 1983, when I was invited to join the Middlesex RFU trip to British Columbia, Canada. Alan Black, who I knew from Wasps, proved to be not only an excellent coach but also an outstanding singer; on that trip, 'Blackie' led singalong after singalong after singalong.

The rugby was hard, but not as challenging for me as the moment when, during a fishing expedition somewhere near Vancouver, our hooker John Olver threw me into the water. We were both wearing life-jackets, but I have never been a strong swimmer and I genuinely thought I was going to drown until a couple of Canadians hauled me out of the sea. John was a good friend from college, who would later win three caps for England, and I remember he was laughing throughout this episode – unfortunately for all of us, I turned out to be just about the only thing anyone caught all day.

The tour concluded with an official dinner by the Waterfront in Vancouver, an occasion made memorable when Andre Dent decided to execute a perfect dive into the harbour, wearing his full Middlesex RFU number ones. Manu Tuilagi, the England centre, performed a similar feat, albeit less well dressed, when he jumped off a ferry into Auckland harbour after the team had been defeated by France in the quarter-final of the 2011 Rugby World Cup. Tuilagi was cautioned by police and fined £3,000 by the RFU. 'Denty' received three cheers. We can see how rugby had evolved in 28 years... not much.

In 1986, the Public School Wanderers followed their declared aim of taking the game to developing nations by arranging a tour to Zimbabwe. The British and Irish Lions tour to South Africa scheduled for that year had been cancelled, so the Wanderers chose a squad drawn from all four nations, and I was delighted to be included. The rugby was hard but the welcome was warm, as we played against Matabeleland, Mashonaland and the national side.

In fact, the welcome was particularly warm for Timmy Bell, the Quins flanker, who spent one night in prison because he had inadvertently walked too close to State House, the home of the then Prime Minister Robert Mugabe. The actual president of Zimbabwe at the time, effectively a ceremonial position, was somebody called Canaan Banana, a fact we all knew because he happened to be travelling on the same flight as us back to London.

In May and June 1987, Middlesex RFU arranged a tour to Australia, brilliantly conceived to coincide with the staging of the very first Rugby World Cup in that part of the world; our squad was apparently chosen by selectors who had been made aware that, in case of injuries, the England World Cup squad could need replacements at very short notice. Some of us might have been much closer to a full international cap than we realised at the time.

We were certainly in excellent form, having memorably defeated Cornwall 20-18 in the semi-final of the County Championship, before eventually losing to Yorkshire in the final at Twickenham on April 11.

The Middlesex team in the final had included a backline of Huw Davies, Simon Smith, Rob Lozowski, C.R.J Smith, Andre Dent, Mark Fletcher and John Cullen at scrum half, and the forwards were Paul Curtis, John Olver, John Thorne, locks Chris Pinnegar and John Howe, Mark Rigby, Ken Moss and Paul Jackson, from Harlequins as captain. I had been selected on the bench, which disappointed me, but, as it turned out, 'JC' was injured and I was brought on as a substitute to play the second half.

In those days, interestingly, eligibility for County teams was based on either where you played your club rugby or where you had been brought up – each player could choose for themselves – and so both Rob Andrew, of Wasps, and John Buckton, of Saracens, started for Yorkshire, where they had been raised.

In any event, the Middlesex squad was feeling strong and confident when we boarded the long flight to Australia. We were guided by the great Dick Best, who would go on to coach England and the 1993 Lions.

Dick was was a wonderful innovator and a brilliant thinker. He was also a demanding taskmaster, who drove us hard, and there were usually more than a few players being sick by the side of the field after one of the fitness sessions that became known as 'Bestie's beastings'. Yet, he ensured we were in great shape and he helped us play some brilliant rugby.

Looking back, I would say Dick Best, Tony Russ and Alan Black were the best three coaches I experienced during my rugby career.

I played the first two matches in Queensland and, after our second win, Dick said: "I didn't know you could play so well, Floyd."

"Well, coach," I replied, "any scrum half can look good when your pack is dominating; that's not always the case at Saracens."

We only lost one match on tour, when we were beaten by a Western Australia team including 14 New Zealanders, and it was a great experience. There was one evening when every single person who was eating in our hotel restaurant ended up in the swimming pool. I think John Olver could have been involved, but I don't remember exactly what happened, which is just as well because, as the old saying goes, what happens on tour stays on tour.

In May 1988, at the end of the English season, Public School Wanderers sent a team to the Monte Carlo Sevens, an event as glamorous as it sounds, and I was pleased to be included as one of two scrum halves in the squad alongside David Kirk, a wonderful player who had only the previous year captained New Zealand to victory in the inaugural Rugby World Cup.

We were sitting in the bar one evening, enjoying a couple of beers, and I remember asking 'Kirkie' what made the All Blacks tick. "First is everything," he replied. Nothing more to be said.

The tournament ended with a glittering formal banquet, after which we found our way to the famous Casino de Monte Carlo, where beers were significantly more expensive than we had anticipated. I was never a heavy drinker, so I was trusted to take charge of the kitty for the night, which meant I was constantly going to ask for more funds from Brigadier Rolph James, legendary President and driving force of the Wanderers for many years.

The rugby life was really not such a bad life. I returned home from Monte Carlo and, barely a week later, was heading back to Heathrow airport, where I joined the Saracens squad assembled for a tour to Quebec, Canada and then Boston, in the United States. It was just one tour after another...

We had entered a tournament, which included four local North American teams and four touring teams, and everything went extremely well: Saracens won the final and took home the trophy, and I was named as what the Americans called the 'MVP', the most valuable player of the tournament.

I loved the approach of the American players. They were getting hammered by the opposition, but they kept getting up, kept trying to make big hits and kept going right until the end. This was the true spirit of rugby.

The last tour of my career, just like the first, was undertaken as a member of the Middlesex squad and, in 1989, we headed to Tunisia. Mark Rigby was tour captain. I was named as his vice-captain, and our coach was Alex Keay, my old friend and teammate from the early days at Saracens.

We had no idea what to expect from the teams in Tunisia, and indeed some members of our squad may have struggled to locate the North African country on a map, but they proved to be big, strong and competitive, similar in many ways to French players, and we worked hard to win both games, one against the national under-23 side and the other against Tunisia.

Once again, the tour offered much more than the rugby... on this occasion, we found ourselves staying in the same hotel as a women's water polo team from West Germany. One thing led to another and these Germans challenged some of the Middlesex rugby players to what became an impromptu game of water polo in the hotel swimming pool. This contest became significantly more fun when the German women opted to remove their tops. Again, as they say in the classics, what happens on tour stays on tour.

Reflecting on these years, it is worth emphasising just how much rugby we played. While modern players may be concerned about playing more than 30 or 35 matches each season, we were regularly playing more than 60 games in one campaign, and nobody ever seemed to complain.

Yes, the game is more physical now but, to repeat, it was more brutal in the 1980s. Yes, modern players are required to train more often than we were, but we were amateurs and most of us also held full-time jobs as well.

I admire the modern players without reservation, and I don't wish to be critical of anybody in any respect, but perhaps there is a difference in mentality – the difference between, on the one hand, people who are being paid to do something and, on the other hand, people doing something they love.

Back in the 1980s, if a player suffered a serious and career-ending injury, it was generally expected that his club would arrange a special match, usually played on a Sunday, to try and raise funds either to pay the player's medical bills or to help him move forward with the rest of his life.

We would be invited to play in these special games, even though we would often have played a club match on the Saturday; and almost always every player would accept the invitation, even if they were feeling tired and sore from playing the previous day.

Why?

Because we all understood the next club player to suffer a serious injury and need a bit of help was going to be one of us.

As much as anything, this general attitude reflected the spirit of our game, the game which I was fortunate to play for so long.

So, by the end of the 1988/89 season, the 'Mickey Mouse' club had won promotion to the First Division of the national leagues, and looked forward to competing with the top clubs in England.

We had arrived. At long last, as Saracens, we were respected.

# Chapter 6

# Frustrated

Roger Uttley was the epitome of an England international rugby player. Tall, strong and brave, kind and generous, usually moustached, he played 23 times for England between 1973 and 1980, either at lock or in the back row, and he excelled in the celebrated British and Irish Lions team that travelled to South Africa in 1974 and defeated the Springboks 3-0.

'Big Rog' was born in Blackpool, where he attended Montgomery High School and Blackpool Grammar School. He progressed to play his club rugby for Fylde in Lancashire, then Gosforth near Newcastle in the north-east before moving to London where he finished his career with Wasps.

He was a member of the famous North side, which defeated the All Blacks at Otley on Saturday 17 November, 1979, and played a prominent role in the England team which won the Grand Slam in 1980. Widely liked and respected throughout the community, he retired from international rugby later that year, aged 31, stepping aside at the pinnacle of the game.

With all this in mind, imagine my excitement when, as an eager youngster in my final year at Kingsbury High School, our coach Brian

Jones nominated me to join a training camp for 'potential England players' to be run by Roger Uttley. For three days, our 'South' group would be coached and trialled at the Bisham Abbey National Sports Centre, west of London.

'Potential England player'? Really?

The concept had scarcely crossed my mind. While many young English boys may have dreamed of wearing the white jersey with the red rose emblem ever since they first touched a ball at primary school, I had grown up in a different world where people barely knew rugby existed.

Was I really 'a potential England player'? I had no idea, but I arrived at Bisham Abbey, listened carefully, tried my best, worked hard, got stuck in, played well and loved every minute of the three days in camp.

"Well done, Floyd," said Roger Uttley at the end of the last day, "you've done really well. Keep working hard and you'll realise your potential."

I started to wonder what that word 'potential' meant for me, whether it might actually be possible for me to play rugby for England. At that time, I was perfectly happy to play for Kingsbury High School and Middlesex Schools but, some time in the future, if I kept working hard, maybe, just maybe...

As it happened, of course, I never played for England. At the time, and looking back after all these years, I felt – and feel – frustrated. I would be lying if I said there were not times, several times, when I felt my performances for club and county merited an opportunity to play for my country.

Why did it not happen?

Well, the simplest explanation is probably the hardest to accept: perhaps I was just not good enough to play international rugby.

A relatively small number of hugely talented, naturally gifted players appear, at any early age, to be equipped to thrive at the highest level; they are stand-out stars at school, and they progress smoothly through representative age-group teams all the way through the system to the national side. Not every member of this elite reaches that highest level. There are no guarantees.

Then, there are a much larger number of talented, gifted players who play for their schools and advance to play for their clubs, and play extremely well, and demonstrate they have the ability to play international rugby, but they only do so if they happen to get the cherished opportunity.

For this second group, the margins are small. An outstanding performance in the right place at the right time, which catches the selectors' eye, or even an injury to a player in the same position can make all the difference. Sometimes the cards fall your way, and sometimes they don't. A few are lucky, many more are not.

I certainly did not fall into the first category but many might have included me in the second group.

People used to call me 'Steady Eddie' because I was consistent. There were days when the game seemed to flow my way, and I would get the ball in dangerous areas, would make a break or score a try, or do something to help us win the game; and, of course, there were also days, mercifully fewer in the number, when the game simply didn't flow my way, for whatever reason, and I was unable to make a significant impact. Some ebb and flow is inevitable but, at all times, above all, I strived to be consistent.

An even level of performance seemed to be particularly important for a player in my position. The scrum half is the fulcrum of the team, the link between the forwards and backs. I set myself certain standards – of playing with energy, communicating effectively, being solid in defence and getting the ball away smoothly and efficiently – and I worked relentlessly hard to ensure that, at worst, I would always maintain these standards.

All that said, perhaps 'Steady Eddie' was always less likely to get the nod from the national selectors than, say, 'Flash Harry'.

There were moments during my career, especially from 1987 onwards, when the long-awaited call seemed imminent. Sometimes a teammate or opponent would say something encouraging in the bar after a match, and I would start to wonder. Other times I would play well, score a try or two, and the writer of the match report would make a passing remark. For a few seasons, the quiet murmur of media speculation seemed to simmer.

For example, Terry O'Connor, the well-respected rugby correspondent of the Daily Mail, wrote a match preview to the 1989 County Championship final at Twickenham, when I captained Middlesex against Lancashire.

"Floyd Steadman could be tempted to forget any plans to retire if he is named in the England squad this season, especially with the 1991 Rugby World Cup not far away," he wrote. "The 31-year-old scrum half will have an outstanding chance to impress the national selectors as he will play in direct opposition to Dewi Morris, who played for England last season."

Middlesex had a strong team for the showpiece final with full back Sean Robinson, hooker John McFarland and No.8 Lee Adamson as the three other Saracens players in the side, and Mike Wedderburn, the Harlequins wing who would later become a Sky Sports news presenter, also providing a serious threat.

However the match was dominated by the large, powerful Lancashire pack of forwards. They laid the platform for an emphatic 32-9 win, and provided Dewi with what is generally known in the game as an armchair ride. He was able to play on the front foot, calling the shots and dictating the game, while I always seemed to be on the back foot, scrambling to get any ball.

Dewi took his opportunity, and deservedly kept his place, and he went on to win 26 England caps between 1988 and 1995.

Was I overlooked by the England rugby selectors because I was black? The answer is not a simple 'yes' or 'no'. Unsurprisingly, the issue is complex.

I believe it is useful to draw a distinction between conscious bias, which can be bluntly defined as overt and undiluted racism, and unconscious bias, which can be more complicated, nuanced and harder to identify.

It is true that I was subjected to conscious bias, even if rarely. There was one particular individual who played for the Met Police and was a teammate at Middlesex. For whatever reason, he used to call me the most terrible racist names whenever he saw me, which was whenever we happened to play in the county team, perhaps four or five times a season.

He wasn't trying to be funny. He was trying to hurt me. What happened to him? Was he warned or cautioned? Was he perhaps even suspended or banned? Nothing happened. In the 1980s, such conduct was tolerated.

It was a fractious period for race relations in Britain. Riots were relatively common and communication between the police and black communities in many areas was poor. Derogatory racist comments about black or Asian immigrants were generally regarded as a legitimate form of everyday humour. Come on, people would say, we're having a bit of laugh. It wasn't funny.

In the sporting world, it became almost commonplace for black professional footballers to be subjected to a chorus of monkey chants from supporters on the terraces whenever they touched the ball.

"Ooo, ooo, ooo."

It was grotesque. At some football clubs, supporters could actually be seen carrying bunches of bananas to the stadium for the sole purpose of throwing them at black players in the visiting team. Nobody stopped them.

Monkey chants were rare at rugby grounds, but I am sorry to say they were not completely unknown. Now and then, at certain clubs, I would be able clearly to hear the chant emanate from somewhere in the stands and terraces.

All that said, I do not believe any selector at any level of the game, let alone a national selector, ever sat down and consciously decided not to pick me for a team because I happened to be black. That was not the nature of the game. That was not the nature of the people involved.

There was, unquestionably, an element of conscious racism in rugby, as there was in almost every area of life. Two matches stand out in my memory, and both happened to have been played between Saracens and Gloucester at Kingsholm.

In my first spell as captain, there was a trio of black players in our team. As we ran out onto the field before the match, I clearly remember hearing a home supporter shout: "Oh my God, there are three of them."

A few years later, playing against the same opponents at the same stadium, when Alex Keay had taken over as captain, several Gloucester forwards tried to put me off my game by making racial remarks. I ignored them. I genuinely was not at all bothered. I had endured many more difficult experiences in my life, and calmly focused on performing as well as possible.

Alex was not so tolerant. He heard exactly what was being said and, to his great credit, decided it was not acceptable. During a break in play, he walked across to the referee and expressed his dissatisfaction.

"Excuse me, sir, have you heard what they are saying to Floyd."

"Well, I'm sure they mean no offence."

"That's not the point, sir. This behaviour is unacceptable, and should not be tolerated in English club rugby. Do you agree?"

"Well, er, yes."

Alex would not back down."Sir, if you do not ask them to stop, and if they do not stop, I am going to take my team off the field."

"I will speak to them."

Tony Bodley, one of the rugby journalists at the time, got wind of what had happened, and called me after the game. I told him exactly what I had heard, just the truth, and the newspapers on the following morning featured headlines declaring: "Steadman accuses Gloucester of racism".

That was not exactly the case, and I did not enjoy the attention. My preference was always to keep my head down and get on with things and, thankfully, that particular story, like most stories, soon blew over.

Such incidents were relatively rare. There were perhaps a dozen occasions when an opponent, or opposing supporter, made any kind of consciously racial remark, and, in my entire career, there was not one single racial incident involving a teammate or supporter of Saracens... not one.

Unconscious bias was, as I say, a more complicated issue.

Is it possible that I was ever not picked for a team because a selector, deep down in his sub-conscious, found it difficult to accept that a black man could be as effective as a white man, particularly in a position such as scrum half, where accurate decision-making and leadership was required?

In all honesty, I believe it was possible.

In such a situation, the selector will not have intended to allow racial factors to impact his judgement, but it would simply have been hard for him, drawing on all his experience within the game, maybe at a private school, a top university and an elite club, on all his knowledge... almost impossible for him to compute a black man could thrive at nine and be the best option.

This would be an example of unconscious bias, and it was as rife in rugby as it was in most sports, workplaces and organisations.

Unconscious bias can only be addressed by education, by providing people with the knowledge to confront and erase such prejudice. Needless to say, nobody in rugby was discussing such matters in the 1980s.

Unconscious bias does not relate only to race.

Is it possible that I was ever not picked for a team because a selector, deep in his sub-conscious, found it difficult to accept a Saracens player could be as talented as a Wasps or a Bath player, especially in a position such as scrum half, where accurate decision-making and leadership was required?

In all honesty, I believe it was possible.

Maybe the opportunity to play for England would have arisen if I had moved to one of the more favoured clubs. Maybe. Nothing is certain. Over the years, I had received a number of tentative approaches from other clubs, but there was nothing tentative about the offer from Bath in 1987.

After a match at the Recreation Ground, I found myself sitting in the bar with Tony Russ, the Saracens coach, and Jack Rowell, the Bath coach, a tall man with a strong sense of presence and purpose; he had coached Bath since 1978 and would eventually guide them through a golden era of 16 years, when they won five league Championships and eight knock-out cups.

"I want you to come to Bath," said Rowell.

"You've already got Richard Hill," I replied, assuming he was joking.

"No, I want you to come to Bath," Rowell repeated.

"Floyd's not going anywhere, Jack," said 'Russy'; in fact, he may have used more colourful language unsuitable for print.

"So will you come?" Rowell persisted, like a man used to getting his way.

"That's very flattering," I replied, eager to be polite, "but my entire life is in London and I will be continuing to play for Saracens."

Would I have played for England if I had moved to Bath? Nobody knows. It doesn't matter. I made my decision, and that was that.

In any event, it was maybe natural, though still not fair, that a selector should unconsciously gravitate towards what he knows, towards what makes him feel reassured and comfortable... towards players of his own colour, towards players from his old school, towards players from his own club etc.

As a black scrum half from a state school playing for Saracens, it did sometimes seem the dice was not loaded in my favour.

Yet, having said all this, I do not want to create the impression that I ever felt as though I was any kind of victim. On the contrary, by and large, and certainly within Saracens, I always felt accepted and welcome, as much a part of club as anybody. In fact, I relished the social side of the game.

As a 23-year-old club captain, in 1981 and 1982, I was expected to speak at functions and to represent the club; I was nervous but there is no doubt I benefited hugely from such experiences.

I was never the most enthusiastic of the drinkers, even though I almost always had a couple of beers after every match and enjoyed Jamaican rum every now and then, but I always preferred to maintain some degree of self-control; this meant that, as at the Monte Carlo Sevens, I was almost always designated as the man trusted to look after the kitty on a night out. A couple of beers and a couple of rums would be enough for me, but that did not prevent me from enjoying myself to the full.

In fairness, we rarely held back. We were amateurs, entitled to receive only travelling expenses, even if they were calculated at what was then a generous rate of around 30 pence per mile. It was understood that the organisation of social events, usually with the club putting more than enough money behind the bar, was an acceptable and allowed form of compensation for the time and effort which we, as players, committed to the game.

Middlesex, in particular, always looked after us. It used to be said that, while some provided jugs of beer, Middlesex could always be expected to provide jugs of gin and tonic.

Our travel expenses were generous. In Wales, they were extraordinary. I remember sitting in the home team changing room after one match, sharing a few beers, and a Welsh club official walked up to the player sitting beside me and passed him a brown envelope stuffed full with notes.

"What's that," I asked innocently.

"Oh, it's just my travel expenses," he explained.

"You must live a long way away," I said.

"No," he said, unblinking. "I live just across the road."

Some people have asked me whether I feel unfortunate to have played in the 'amateur' era, and perhaps to have missed out on the hundreds of thousands of pounds which are paid to leading players today.

My response is always the same: I don't feel unlucky at all. It was a different era in the 1980s, with a different rewards structure; we may have received nothing in our bank accounts, but we were richer in other ways.

In all honesty, I reflect on my rugby career with no regrets, no regrets at all. I may not have been the epitome of an English international rugby player. I may have come from a different background and looked different from most of my teammates, but I felt accepted and at home within the game.

Even so, it's a fact that I never had the opportunity to play for England, and it's a fact that, even now, decades later, I still feel slightly frustrated.

# Chapter 7

# Praised

Towards the end of the 1988/89 season, as our promotion to Division One of the national leagues became a reality, I started to wonder whether this was not the right moment to step aside and retire. I was increasingly busy both at work in school and at home, and it was becoming harder and harder for me to find enough hours in the day to meet all my commitments.

"Come on, Floydy, just one more season," teammates said.

I certainly didn't want to let anybody down, but I was not sure. I had hurt my knee during a match against Nuneaton in a Cup match the previous season, and the doctor had told me in no uncertain terms that enough is enough. If you cause any more damage, he said, you may not walk again. I had already endured keyhole surgery on my knee, but it's a strange fact that rugby players seem to have a problem hearing what doctors say.

The decision when to retire seemed more simple in those days, than it has become today. Back in the 1980s, there was the issue of being physically fit and seeking to preserve future health, but the main factor in the decision was simply whether you had had enough of the training, travelling and playing.

Retirement had virtually no impact on your financial position or your personal life because you were, in any event, working and earning nothing from the game; in fact, if there was any impact, it would be positive because you would have more time to spend at work and with the family.

The retirement process is much more challenging for modern players because they must face up to the reality that (a) they will be compelled to transition into a second career, for which many are unprepared, and (b) they will have to deal with a substantial reduction in household income.

What seemed straightforward in 1989 can seem traumatic today.

"Come on, Floydy, just one more season."

"OK, just one more, but that will definitely be enough for me."

So I threw myself into pre-season training, and looked forward to the challenge of leading Saracens into Division One. George Sherriff had been elected as club President, and I was asked to continue as club captain.

There was the usual shuffling of the pack before the season started, with Dean Ryan becoming the latest Saracens player to be poached by Wasps. There was nothing we could do to change the fact that talented young players would often make their mark at Bramley Road, and then be lured away to play for the more reputable and maybe more fashionable London clubs.

All we could do was go and find yet another talented young player and, when Dean left, that is precisely what we did.

Somebody had told me about a promising 21-year-old number eight playing for Bishop's Stortford RFC in Hertfordshire, named Ben Clarke. I called a few people and the reports were outstanding. I spoke to Tony Russ, and we agreed I should contact the youngster and invite him to join us. As it happened, he was travelling in Australia at the time, but I persisted and eventually managed to get him on the end of a crackly telephone line.

"Hello, Ben, this is Floyd Steadman, from Saracens."

"Who? What?"

I eventually conveyed what I wanted to say and, sure enough, as soon as he returned from his trip, Clarkey turned up at Saracens. He was put straight into the first team, scored a try on his debut and more than adequately filled the gap left by Dean at the back of the scrum.

With all modesty, it was an excellent piece of recruitment. Ben would go on to enjoy an outstanding rugby career, playing for Bath, Richmond, Bath again and finally Worcester Warriors; he won 40 caps for England and played one Test for the British Lions on the 1993 tour to New Zealand.

We also welcomed a dynamic young flanker from Southend RFC, called Chris Tarbuck. Alan Phillips was already at the club and, together, Clarke, Tarbuck and Phillips would form a youthful, mobile and effective trio of loose forwards, who tackled anything and everything that moved in an opposition jersey, and who would become central to our gameplan.

Mark Evans was another significant arrival. He was a useful hooker who had played for Saracens before moving across to Blackheath but he returned to Bramley Road in the summer of 1989 to start his coaching career, becoming an assistant in an impressive unit under Tony Russ.

Clever and resourceful, Mark has an exceptional rugby brain. He understands every aspect of the game, and had made a huge contribution, initially as the Director of Rugby at Saracens at the start of the professional era and then as Chief Executive of Harlequins between 2000 and 2011. He would also enjoy great success as CEO of the Melbourne Storm rugby league team.

None of his achievements have surprised me, although I may not qualify as a completely impartial witness because Mark was and remains close friend, and I was delighted when he agreed to write the Foreword to this book.

As the 1989/90 season approached, our squad began to take shape. We had retained the core of the team that had so impressively won promotion, keeping faith with a group of relatively young, fit players who enjoyed playing for the club and, as importantly, enjoyed playing with each other, together with one or two experienced players, such as the 31-year-old at scrum half.

Sean Robinson was still excelling as a running full back, and our backline was built around the top quality midfield combination of the stampeding Laurence Smith at 12 and the speed and silky skills of John Buckton at 13. Ben Rudling and Martyn Gregory also excelled, and Andy Kennedy emerged as one of the most accurate goal kickers in the league with a success percentage that compared with the celebrated Dusty Hare, of Leicester and England.

I watched this backline in pre-season and felt excited. If we could get enough possession up front, we had players capable of moving the ball at speed and quite literally running the opposition off the park.

Our forwards were talented, strong and mobile, and no fewer than five of the starting pack were younger than 23 at the start of the season. Would they be able to hold their ground and meet the challenge presented by older, wiser, more experienced, maybe even more gnarled and cynical packs? This was the key question. Our hopes hung on the answer being 'yes'.

Club rugby in England was evolving. The process had been accelerated by the introduction of the national leagues and our weekly routine in 1989/90 was unrecognisable from 1980, when I started. Where once we were invited to turn up to training only on Tuesday and Thursday evenings, now we were expected to do something almost every day of the week.

Nobody complained. We wanted to do more. Tony and Mark were imaginative and innovative coaches, ahead of their time, always looking for a different, better way of doing things, and we eagerly responded.

After playing a match on the Saturday, we were all encouraged to go for a gentle run on the Sunday and a gym session on the Monday, either on our own or with a few teammates. Fitness was not a problem for me because, as a PE teacher, I spent most days in a gym.

A full squad training on the Tuesday evening was followed by a track session on the Wednesday, when we would gather at an athletics stadium in Tottenham and get through some serious running. After work on Thursday, we would be back at Bramley Road for another squad training session. Friday was invariably free, and we were told to rest before the match on Saturday.

Looking back, and bearing in mind we were all holding down full-time jobs as well, perhaps the main difference between us and professional players was that we were being paid our 'generous' travel expenses as opposed to a full time salary.

A sense of optimism was growing within the club, even among the committee, who anticipated a surge in support and developed plans to install temporary stands and increase the 2,500 capacity at Bramley Road. Sadly, the excitement did not extend to the council, who rejected the application.

Further afield, around the country, the general consensus was that Saracens would be relegated straight back to Division Two, from where we had come. A series of season previews appeared in the newspapers, suggesting our inexperienced pack of forwards would be exposed and that we would simply be overpowered and overrun by the juggernaut clubs.

"We're being written off," Tony Russ told us, masterfully using the prophets of doom as motivation. "We'll catch them all by surprise."

Bedford had also been promoted to the First Division, and the opening match of our league season – away to Bedford at Goldington Road – felt like a useful indicator of which of the new clubs would sink or swim. We swam, performing with accuracy and speed, and scored five tries in a 22-3 victory. Bedford sunk, going on to lose all 11 league matches and be relegated.

Orrell were the first visitors of the league season to Bramley Road, and the obvious discomfort of the northern powerhouse team when they arrived and looked around was wonderful to see. Strange as it may seem, dog walkers were entitled to roam around our home ground during the week, and match day began with a ritual exercise where people with spades would scour the first team pitch and scoop away what the dogs had left behind.

They had hoped their heavyweight pack would bludgeon us into submission, with the talented England scrum half Dewi Morris snapping and sniping from the back of the scrum, but we made every tackle, and we ran and ran and ran until these big men from the north were exhausted, bent double, blowing hard, with their hands resting on their knees.

'Bucko' executed an intercept. He sprinted at least 80 yards, almost the length of the field, and scored what proved to be the only try of the game. Roared on by the home supporters, we hung on to win 12-6. The post-match jugs of beer arrived in our changing room and tasted better than ever. Who said we were relegation candidates? We had won two from two.

Tony Russ was intelligently guiding us through the campaign, for the first time unashamedly prioritising league matches over friendlies in our fixture list, and ensuring that our leading players were primed and prepared to perform when it really mattered. If the coach felt it was necessary to put out a younger team against the likes of Newport or Ebbw Vale, he did so.

We were beaten fair and square away at Nottingham, a powerful team which included a talented young hooker by the name of Brian Moore, but we refused to panic, regrouped and bounced back to post a magnificent 33-13 win over Moseley at Bramley Road on Saturday 28 October.

The match report in the Daily Mail concluded: "Saracens started the season worrying about a struggle to avoid relegation, but this excellent victory means the buoyant north London club can mount a title challenge."

The Daily Express reflected: "Floyd Steadman could almost be described as the Sebastian Coe of Saracens. He's the ultimate ambassador for both his club and for the game of rugby. When Floyd joined Saracens at the start of the 1980s, the club was at its lowest ebb for many years. He was flung in at the deep end into captaincy and the tide slowly began to turn. Alex Keay and then Lee Adamson led the club, before Floyd returned as captain last year. The club has now started to reap the reward of many years of hard work."

Everyone enjoys reading such praise in the newspapers, but we were brought back down to earth in our next league match at Welford Road. The final score was Leicester 34 Saracens 5, a thumping which meant we had suffered 22 consecutive defeats to the Tigers.

They were exceptionally strong, with the Underwood brothers, Rory and Tony, on the wings, the wily Les Cusworth pulling the strings at 10, and flanker Ian Smith, who people used to call 'Dosser', dominating the loose. My memories of this game are painful. To be honest, it felt like men against boys.

Some pundits suggested the young Saracens team had peaked and that their campaign would unravel with tough matches to come at home to Harlequins and away to Gloucester. It seemed our season would be defined in the space of eight days in October.

Quins were universally expected to win, not least by themselves, and underpin their own challenge for the title, but we rose to the occasion and I managed to produce what I recall as perhaps one of the most effective performances of my career. They were skilful and strong, but we stayed in the game, tackling with energy, moving the ball wide at every opportunity.

There was never much more than one score between the teams and, midway through the second half, we won a scrum five metres from their line. This was my opportunity, I thought, and I decided I would take the ball and make a dart to score, using my strength and low centre of gravity to find a way through the Harlequins defence and burrow my way to the line.

Everything seemed to happen in slow motion. I took the ball and glanced up to see the imposing figure of Mickey Skinner standing immediately in front of me, a man mountain between me and the try line. There was a sound reason why he was known as 'Mick the Munch', and that was his ability to swallow up opponents in what were often awe-inspiring tackles.

If I was going to have any chance, I would have to go low; and, summoning every ounce of strength, straining every sinew, I managed to generate some momentum, keep hold of the ball and wriggle over the line. The referee blew his whistle and raised his hand to signal the try.

'Saracens 15 Harlequins 9' read the wooden scoreboard at full time, and a record crowd of 1,800 saluted a famous win.

I was delighted, of course, but there was no maniacal leaping around in victory in those days and, after the end of the match, I calmly approached the Harlequins captain on the day and offered to shake his hand. He declined. He apologised later, of course, but his reaction reflected the depth of their frustration.

In that moment, it was obvious that we were getting under their skin. We had emerged from the shadows, at last. We were winning major matches. Saracens were becoming a genuine force in English club rugby.

Tony Russ spoke in the changing room afterwards. "Enjoy the win tonight but please don't go overboard," the coach said. "People are talking about us. Let's make sure we're ready for Kingsholm next weekend."

Gloucester away was a significant challenge and, for an hour, it seemed likely to end in the same humbling outcome as the trips to

Nottingham and Leicester. We were trailing 6-17, and apparently headed for another defeat on the road, a young team unable to cope with the heavy traffic. Something stirred in the last quarter, and we somehow found a foothold in the game. We refused to roll over. We kept working hard, kept making tackles, kept running, kept our heads under pressure, kept making wise decisions.

It felt fantastic to stay together, and to stay in the fight.

"Floyd, I'm sure I can hear Carol's voice. Can you hear her?"

"What?"

"I said I am sure I can hear Carol's voice."

"What on earth are you talking about?"

In the midst of this intense struggle, maybe the most exhilarating match of our entire season, John Buckton had walked over to me and told me that, amid all the noise coming from the Shed, the terrace where the most vocal and committed Gloucester supporters chose to stand, he could hear his girlfriend.

"Bucko, what do you mean?"

"Floyd, I'm telling you I can hear Carol. I am serious," he insisted.

He was pointing to one particular area of the ground and, during a break in play, we stood together and scanned the rows of faces. Sure enough, there she was. Completely unbeknown to us, Carol Buckton, my wife Denise and several wives and girlfriends of other players had travelled to support us in Gloucester. They had wanted to surprise us. They certainly did.

"Well, I suppose we had better do something about the scoreline," Bucko said with a grin, as we took our places for the next play.

The tide began to turn. John scored a try, but Gloucester hit back. Then Sean Robinson scored a try. With barely a few seconds remaining, we trailed 15-21, and seemed destined to finish as gallant losers. There was time for one more move, one more surge. The ball found its way to Ben Clarke, who surged past two flailing defenders and managed to score in the corner.

In an instant, the Shed fell silent. There was only time left for Andy Kennedy to attempt a conversion from the touchline, which would level the scores at 21-21 and secure the draw. 'AK' prepared, steadied, moved towards the ball, made a sweet connection and sent the ball between the posts. Never in my experience has a draw ever felt so much like a glorious victory.

Kingsholm was momentarily stunned but, to their great credit, the Gloucester players and supporters were good value in the bar afterwards, buying us more than a few beers, congratulating us on our extraordinary fightback, pleased to celebrate what had been a great, great game of rugby. With some of our wives and girlfriends present, we could not have been happier.

There were no league matches in November and December, but we continued playing friendlies until, on January 13, we resumed our campaign with a 17-12 win over Bristol at Bramley Road.

Once again people had started to ask me whether I was planning to retire at the end of the season, and I was grateful to Tony Russ, who attempted to draw a line beneath the issue when he told journalists: "I believe we will lose Floyd this year. It will be a huge blow, particularly for me, because we have worked together since I arrived seven years ago. He's my voice on the field. He reads the game well and the whole side respects him."

I tried to confirm my intentions, explaining: "Training nights make it a long hard day for me. I drive into London at seven in the morning and then out to Saracens and back home to Ealing. I am still enjoying my rugby, but I like to see my wife occasionally and I've had a good run."

Soon afterwards, it was announced that Tony Russ would also be leaving the club at the end of the season to start work as Director of Rugby at Leicester. The imminent departures of coach and captain could have proved a distraction, but that lay ahead in the future and we resolved to stay focused on the present.

Three league matches remained and, strange but true, if we won all three, and if a few other results fell our way, it was mathematically possible for Saracens, formed in 1876, to finish in first place and be crowned English club champions for the very first time in our long 114-year history.

The campaign was becoming a fairytale.

Rosslyn Park came to Bramley Road on Saturday 10 March, and seemed to be edging towards a narrow victory, until we won a penalty in the last minute of the match. The ball was thrown to Andy Lee, who was playing his debut for us at fly half. He had played cricket for Essex juniors and, coping admirably with the pressure, he kicked the goal to snatch a 15-13 win.

Around 3,000 spectators celebrated another home victory. At the start of the season, a crowd of this size had seemed unimaginable. Now our friends at the council were imposing a limit on our attendances. Residents living around the ground had started to complain about noise. As a club, on and off the field, in so many ways, we were moving into uncharted waters.

Three weeks later, on Saturday 31 March, we were back at Bramley Road to play against Bath, who were also competing for the title.

Under usual circumstances, a scrum half as captain would pick a vice-captain from among the forwards but, at the start of the season, I had gone down a different route and invited our full back, Sean Robinson, to be vice-captain. There seemed to be enough natural leaders among the pack who did not need the title, and Sean enjoyed the extra responsibility, especially when we played against Bath, a team captained by his brother Andy.

A close and competitive contest ensued. We had withstood periods of intense pressure from powerful opponents and somehow stayed in contention, but Bath led 7-3 with five minutes to play.

Almost out of the blue, Andy Lee took the ball and burst down the left wing to score a try that pulled us level at 7-7. Yet another home match in this special season was hurtling towards yet another dramatic conclusion.

There was just time for us to attempt the conversion to Andy's try, and so to win the match. It was far from an easy kick, and I opted to throw the ball to my unusual choice as vice-captain. Sean nodded, accepted the challenge, moved through his process and kicked the extra points. Bedlam broke out in the grandstand. Once again, Saracens supporters, old and new, were celebrating.

The win over Bath meant that, with the only last round of league fixtures still to be played on Saturday 28 April, 1990, only three clubs – Wasps, Gloucester and Saracens – could mathematically still win the title. Our eleventh and final league match would be played away to Wasps at Sudbury.

A significantly inferior points difference meant our chance was purely mathematical, but the fact remains we had stayed in contention until the final weekend of the league season, and that was a fantastic achievement for a club which so many had predicted would be relegated. The respective rugby writers at the time were almost united in their praise for the manner in which we had approached the season and the way we had performed.

"Saracens have set a fine example for other ambitious clubs to follow," ran one report in the Daily Express. "They have only added junior club players to the squad that won promotion last year. They did not go into the transfer market to buy proven First Division performers, yet they have been able to take on the best of the top flight and win. This approach contrasts to others who offer jobs, accommodation and travel expenses to attract new faces."

Our final home match of the season – the last home match of my career – was a friendly against Liverpool St Helens at Bramley Road on the weekend before the concluding league match at Wasps, and an emotional occasion ended in a defeat, as we conceded two late tries and lost 16-24.

Everybody was extremely kind and generous. "The records will show it was Steadman's commitment and enthusiasm which set in motion the Saracens revival of the 1980s," said the Daily Telegraph.

So we travelled to Sudbury for our last league match, and the last competitive match of my rugby career, eager to end the season on a high note. We faced a Wasps team determined to win the title themselves and, in truth, the outcome was never in doubt from only the second minute of the match, when their pack found some momentum and Mark Rigby scored a pushover try.

Rob Andrew, the England fly half, took control of the game and expertly steered Wasps to an emphatic win. We never gave up and kept fighting, and I was able to scramble over the line and score one last try from short range towards the end of the second half, as we succumbed to a 24-6 defeat.

A strange hiatus followed the final whistle at Sudbury until, after what seemed like several minutes, news was received that Gloucester had lost their match at Nottingham and Wasps were confirmed as league champions.

They deserved their success and, with people wearing black-and-gold starting to celebrate in and around the clubhouse, I spoke to some journalists. "London rugby, as a whole, can be very proud of their achievement," I said. "They have been the most consistent and impressive team all year."

More media plaudits followed.

Chris Jones, of the Evening Standard, wrote: "The Wasps crowd, on a high by this time, greeted Steadman's late try with delight, showing that sentiment is not dead yet even at this pretty high grade of rugby."

Ian Malin, of The Guardian, wrote: "The game will miss Steadman. Had the former Wasps colt decided to stay at Sudbury all those years ago, he would surely have become an England scrum half."

Barrie Fairall, of the Independent, wrote: "So Steadman retires from rugby as surely one of the best never to have played for England."

I appreciated the compliments, but never felt comfortable as the focus of attention and preferred to get changed, enjoy a few quiet beers, throw my bag into the boot of my car one last time and drive home... happy and content to have played what someone told me had been my 465th, and final, appearance for Saracens.

Towards the end of my last season, in March 1990, I was invited to play for the Barbarians against East Midlands in the annual Mobbs

Memorial match, played at Franklin's Gardens in Northampton. It was a significant honour for me, and I was thrilled.

Almost all the finest players in the game had at some stage been invited to play for the Baabaas, and this was an invitation rarely declined. Some said my selection could be interpreted as an unofficial consolation for missing out on a chance to play for England. I didn't know. As far as I was concerned, I felt as though, in some way, I was being accepted into an elite.

The Barbarian Football Club was formed in 1890 by William Percy Carpmael, an advocate of short tours as an important element of the game. The club was given its motto by Walter Carey, a member and a former Bishop of Bloemfontein, as follows: "Rugby football is a game for gentlemen in all classes, but for no bad sportsman in any class."

Traditions evolved. The Barbarians wore the famous black-and-white hooped jerseys, but each player wore the socks of his home club. Squads would be invited from across the world for each tour or match, and each team would include at least one uncapped player. When the players gathered, as much bonding and match preparation would take place in the bar as on the training field.

A mythology grew around the club following the match against the All Blacks in Cardiff in 1973, when Phil Bennett executed two sidesteps in front of his own posts and launched a move which flowed the length of the field and ended with Gareth Edwards scoring maybe the greatest of all tries. "What a score," Cliff Morgan, the BBC commentator, famously exclaimed.

Barbarian teams were expected to move the ball around, entertain and to be, in effect, the Harlem Globetrotters of rugby.

Les Cusworth, of England, was picked at fly half, with me at scrum half, in an accomplished side drawn from all corners of the United Kingdom, including wing Tony Underwood, of England, lock Neil Francis, of Ireland, prop Paul Burnell, of Scotland, and prop Mike Griffiths, of Wales.

As often happened with hastily assembled Barbarian teams, we struggled to settle and find any momentum in the first half and trailed the East Midlands 18-4 at half-time. Micky Steele-Bodger, much loved President of the club, would later recall he was extremely troubled because he had only recently agreed the club's first ever sponsorship deal with Scottish Amicable, a life insurer, and, as he said, he was "afraid they would want their money back."

In the event, we found some rhythm in the second half and scored 36 points without reply, and eventually won the match 40-18. I managed to score one of our tries, spotting a gap, taking a quick tap penalty and making what had become one of my trademarks bursts over the line.

Playing for the Barbarians was the cherry on the cake of what seemed at the time, and seems on reflection, to have been possibly the perfect final season of my career. I could not have wished for anything more.

I had arrived at Saracens at the start of the 1980/81 season, just as the club was about to endure one of the most disappointing seasons in its history, and I played for ten consecutive seasons, leaving at the end of 1989/90, with the club just one win away from being English champions.

This extraordinary progress was made possible by the remarkable efforts of many people, on and off the field, and I was pleased to have played a small part in the development of a club which I will always love.

However, in closing, looking back after all these years, I want to pay tribute to the lead architect of our success, Tony Russ. More than anybody, he was the man who laid the plans, who motivated and inspired.

Born in Birkenhead, a schoolmaster by profession, 'Russy' had arrived at Saracens in 1984 and discovered a club ethos exemplified by the behaviour of an unnamed first team player, who used regularly to arrive at training on a Tuesday evening and sit quietly in his car until he was absolutely sure the demanding fitness session had ended and only then emerge, smiling, apologising for being late, declaring "the traffic on the M25 was terrible".

By 1989/90, such conduct was simply unimaginable for any member of the bright, fit, determined, young squad that performed so well in the First Division.

As much as anything, that is the most accurate measure of Russy's progress, of our progress. He, and we, were rightly praised.

# Chapter 8

# Employed

So often in my life, somebody has said: "no, you can't do that". So often, I said nothing in reply, preferring to put my head down and work harder. So often, quietly, I said to myself: "yes, I can."

Somebody said I can't get decent O levels. I said I can. Somebody said I can't stay at school and take A levels. I said I can. Somebody said work with your hands because you will never be a teacher. I said I can.

In truth, I had not always wanted to be a teacher. When I was 10 years old, a natural inclination to be structured and organised meant I set my heart on becoming the curator of a museum, an unusual boyhood ambition. I loved collecting things, enjoyed cataloguing them and displaying them on the shelf of the small shed in Uncle Bill and Aunt Betty's garden. It didn't matter that these items were essentially worthless: stones, coins and household debris. This was my collection in my museum, and I was the curator.

The teaching bug bit me as soon as I met Brian Jones, the physical education teacher at Kingsbury High School who introduced me to rugby. I watched him closely, watched him work, organise, motivate and inspire... and decided, at the age of 14, that I wanted to grow up and be like Mr Jones.

I wanted to be a PE teacher: no ifs, no buts, no doubts.

That became my clear and overriding goal. Every question became simple. If it helped me become a teacher, the answer was yes. If it didn't help me become a teacher, the answer was no. For example, should I (a) find a job at 16 or (b) stay at school to study A levels? I needed A levels to get into teacher training college. Answer B: stay at school. Final answer.

"OK, Floyd," one of older, more experienced teachers at Kingsbury told me, "you need to be realistic. It may be better for you to train as a car mechanic like your father. Or learn to be a carpenter. There are many youngsters in the Caribbean community who have done well in jobs like that."

"Thank you, sir," I replied.

Answer B: stay at school and study A levels. Final answer. I was insistent because, even at a young age, I recognised education was the vehicle which would enable me to break through what was considered 'normal' for young black boys like me. With an education, there would be almost no limit. Without an education, there would be almost no chance.

I persisted. The teachers relented. I passed my A levels, and gained entry to the teacher training course at Borough Road College.

That sentence is so easy to write... "I passed my A levels, and gained entry to the teacher training course at Borough Road College". It's just 17 words. And yet the achievement outlined in these 17 words was precisely what enabled a looked-after black teenager to live a life of purpose.

I know this observation may come across as dull and uninspiring, but it is so important. I urge young people, whatever anyone

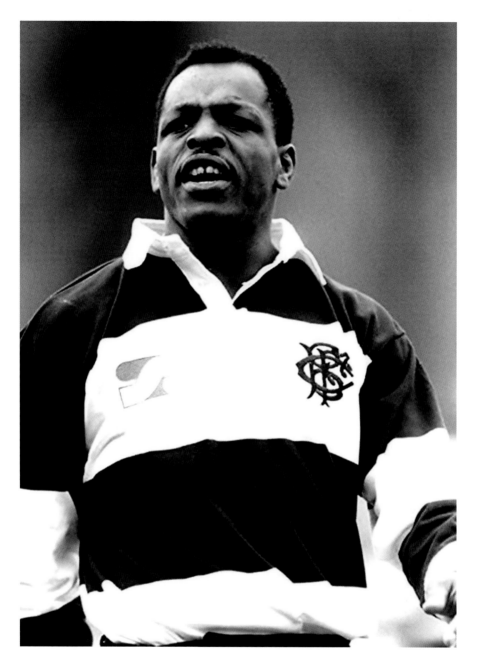

England selection never materialised for me, despite occasional media speculation, but I was extremely pleased and proud to be invited to play for the Barbarians against the East Midlands in 1990.

Saracens were promoted at the end of 1988/89 and challenged for the First Division title in the following season. *Above*, we enjoyed many happy days with our supporters at Bramley Road and, *below*, I clear our lines playing against Wasps at Sudbury, with referee Clive Griffiths in red.

We lost the last match of the 1989/90 season, and the final match of my career, the title-decider away at Wasps. *Above*, our young prop Jason Leonard, helps me out at the breakdown and, *below*, I tackle Wasps hooker Alan Simmons, with Rob Andrew, left, looking on.

*Above*, teaching a trampoline class at Bishop Douglass School in 1987. *Below left*, Derek Rosenberg, who helped me so much as a teacher, receives his MBE. *Below right*, I was delighted with my appointment as Headmaster at Cumnor House School in 2017.

I was extremely fortunate to meet Denise Friggens, *above*, when we studied together at Borough Road College, and made the best decision of my life when I asked her to become my wife. Thank goodness she said 'yes', and we were married in Cornwall on August 6, 1983, *below*.

We enjoyed posing for this happy family portrait in 2001, with our young sons Lewis, Josh and Ollie, *above*, though we were severely outnumbered by Denise, her mother and seven sisters, *below*, from left to right, Denise, Sally, Sue, Liz, mother Joan, Angela, Caroline, Mandy and Janet.

*Above,* At Land's End, Denise and I with her mother Joan and father Dennis, our nephew Ryan Westren and nieces Amy Clemens (née Dann) and Kate Laity (née Dann). *Below,* At home with friends, left to right, John Glover, Jen Moseley, me, Sonja Vio, Denise, Pat Murphy and Debbie Chetwyn.

I am enormously proud of my three sons, Josh, Ollie and Lewis.

ever tells them, whatever their circumstances, whatever their ambitions – always insist and persist and, if necessary, fight for the right to be educated.

In the early summer of 1980, I completed three years at college and emerged with what was known in those days as a 'Cert Ed', a Certificate of Education, the professional qualification required for teachers wanting to work in primary schools or high schools in the United Kingdom.

Bev Risman, my rugby coach at Borough Road, had proposed that I apply to study land economy at Oxford University, with the aim of playing in the Varsity match and winning a 'Blue'. Land economy was the degree of preference for talented sportsmen in those days, but I was eager to find a job, and to start earning a living, and to move on with my life.

On Saturday 3 May, 1980, Borough Road College was one of 16 teams invited to compete in the Middlesex Sevens at Twickenham. It was always a wonderful event, and drew a boisterous crowd of 50,000 to the home of English rugby. It was a knock-out tournament in those days and, on this occasion, we lost our first round match to Richmond, the eventual winners.

A relaxed, good-natured crowd of a few hundred people were milling around the area set aside for participating teams and their friends. Everyone seemed happy, sinking a few beers in the warm, spring sunshine.

"Steadman, I hear you want to be a teacher," said a voice in the crowd.

I turned around and saw a tall, smiling gentleman wearing glasses, enjoying his day at the rugby. He looked familiar. Almost everyone knew everyone on the club rugby circuit in north and west London, and I was able to place him as one of the more prominent members of Hendon RFC.

"Yes, that's right," I replied, smiling.

"Well, there's a position coming up at my school and you should apply," he said, before being distracted by a friend who was shouting at him from the bar, asking what he wanted to drink.

"OK, thanks," I said, and that was that. The tall man seemed friendly enough, but I didn't think much more about the suggestion, offered towards the end of a long day, after which memories would be hazy at best.

Time passed until the end of my course. I needed to find a job, and I began ever more urgently to scour the pages of The Times Educational Supplement, the weekly publication where teaching jobs were advertised. For aspiring teachers, TES was the gateway to the future.

Week after week, I would look through the vacancies, and apply for any job so long as it met one condition. The school needed to be within travelling distance of Bramley Road, so I could attend evening training at Saracens.

I sent application after application, and usually received a response. Most said 'thanks, but no thanks' until, at the end of May, I was invited to attend an interview for a junior PE teacher job at Edgware School. The opportunity seemed ideal.

Dressed in a jacket and tie, I reported to school reception ahead of the appointed time. It was an important moment. I needed to secure my first proper job, and I was shaking with nerves when I sat in a meeting room, waiting for my interviewer to arrive.

The door opened... I looked up... and immediately recognised the tall, smiling gentleman wearing glasses.

"Well, good morning, Floyd," he said warmly, putting me at ease. "It's good to see you again. How did Saracens go at the weekend?"

His name was Derek Rosenberg, Head of Physical Education. We chatted about rugby, about what I wanted to do in my career and about the school. After 40 minutes, he explained I would still need to have a formal chat with the headmaster but implied it would be a formality. So far as I could see, I had secured my first full-time job, and my first monthly salary.

Like my house parents Uncle Bill and Aunt Betty, like my rugby coach Brian Jones, and like my close friend Gareth James, Derek became one of a special group of people who arrived in my life just when I needed a break, who saw something in me, who supported me and who loved me.

Derek was a South African by birth. His father had been closely associated with Nelson Mandela and other African National Congress leaders in the 1950s and early 1960s, and had been one of a notable group of white South African Jews who had the courage to stand up and oppose the apartheid regime.

Mandela was, and remains, one of my personal heroes, not least because he has always championed the cause of education. In his brilliant autobiography 'Long Walk to Freedom', he acknowledged the role played by people such as Derek's father, Joe Slovo, Ruth First, Dennis Goldberg, Albie Sachs, Helen Suzman and many others. Madiba wrote: "I have often found Jews to be more broadminded than most whites on issues of race and politics, perhaps because they themselves have historically been victims of prejudice."

In the early 1960s, the South African police started to crack down ruthlessly on those regarded as dissidents. The likes of Mandela, Walter Sisulu and others were arrested, accused in the notorious Rivonia treason trials and sent to serve prison sentences on Robben Island, near Cape Town.

The Rosenberg family were also threatened, and Derek's father had decided it was necessary for him, his wife and young children initially to flee to Swaziland for three months. When his parents returned to Johannesburg, Derek stayed in the independent kingdom, and attended what was the first multi-racial school in southern Africa alongside the likes of Trevor Tutu, first son of the Archbishop Desmond, and Ian Khama, future president of Botswana.

The family eventually travelled to England in 1969, escaping from South Africa on what was called an exit permit, which meant Derek's parents were permitted to leave but faced prison if they ever returned. They set about the challenge of building a new life in London, effectively in exile.

My first boss was the product of such a remarkable family and of such remarkable experiences. It was, therefore, maybe not surprising that he was able to see the potential in the young black man sitting in front of him, shaking with nerves, on that afternoon in north London, and to give me a chance.

Derek was a lovely, lovely man, a keen sportsman who enjoyed his rugby at Hendon. He climbed mountains and became such a talented canoe surfer that he represented Great Britain in the sport. He demanded high standards, and he could be tough if necessary, but I cannot exaggerate how much I learned in four years spent working for him at Edgware School.

My teaching career did not have the most comfortable start. I arrived at school for my first day, thinking I looked quite smart in a jumper, a shirt and tie and a smart pair of trousers, and I was feeling positive as I walked across to join my allocated class, when someone began yelling.

"Excuse me! Where are you going? Where are your friends?"

One of the older teachers was barking instructions. I looked around to see who he was shouting at, and couldn't see anybody.

"I mean, you," he shouted, staring directly at me. "Where are you going."

I suppose I was relatively short, but I was also stocky, much stockier than the average 17-year-old. So I walked over to him, and explained I was actually a new teacher, not a pupil. He muttered an apology, and sheepishly asked if he could point me in the right direction. I said I was fine.

Edgware School could have been described as 'challenging' at the time, and Derek told me he felt more rugby at the school would provide the pupils with a safer and more structured outlet for their energy. He explained his vision, and asked me to help him put it into practice.

We started teaching basic rugby skills in PE lessons, and the plan started to yield dividends. Football and athletics were the most popular sports at school, and Edgware each year sent around eight or nine talented youngsters to the national athletics championships, but rugby began to grow.

Derek and I became known as the 'rugby guys'. Whenever a fight broke out, the 'rugby guys' would be called to resolve the situation. On one occasion, a stressed 16-year-old lost control in a woodwork class and was threatening people with a hack-saw. The 'rugby guys' were summoned. I tried to placate the youngster, but he took a swing at me and cut my arm. It was difficult, but peace was soon restored.

I was learning. When students were aggressive, I needed to stay calm. If they became more aggressive, I needed to be even more calm. If students were rude, I needed to be polite back to them. "They're not being rude to you as a person," Derek told me, "they're being rude to the system."

Week by week at Edgware School, he taught me to be a teacher.

One morning, just before Christmas, we arrived to find the school blanketed by snow. Derek was extremely excited. He approached six teachers and told us he wanted us to attack the students with snowballs. He said we could catch them by surprise and ambush them during the morning break.

"Are you serious?"

"Absolutely," he replied, smiling broadly.

"There will be a thousand students, and six of us."

"That's why we must catch them by surprise," he said.

Derek's plan failed. Six of us began throwing snowballs. The students threw snowballs back at us, and, to be fair, we were destroyed. It was carnage. At one stage, I was cowering in a corner while 40 exhilarated students enjoyed the free pass to pelt a teacher with snowballs.

We retreated to the staff room. Derek was still smiling. "That was brilliant," he said. "That's exactly the kind of relationship we need to have with these young people. We can't run this school like dictators. There must be times when, in safe circumstances, they can give us stick."

Derek started work at Edgware School in September 1974, and he would serve as Head of PE for 35 years and four months. He worked through the relaunch of the school as the London Academy in 2004, finally retired in December 2009, and was deservedly made an MBE, a Member of the British Empire, in the New Year's Honours list of 2011, being cited for 'services to physical education in the London Borough of Barnet'.

I did not work for quite as long at Edgware School.

In fact, in 1984, after four rewarding years, I was pulled aside by Derek, who told me I should move on. He said I was good enough to be running my own department and thought that, rather than wait for someone to leave or retire at Edgware, I should actively look for a more senior position at another school, where I would be given greater responsibility.

Once again, I had reason to be grateful to this extraordinary man. He had given me my first job and taught me so much and now, thinking only of me and not himself, he was offering timely advice.

I started to look around, and was interested to hear Richard Grey, a senior PE teacher at the Bishop Douglass Catholic School, in East Finchley, had accepted a new position as the new Director of Sport in Barnet. You should go for my old job, he told me, it's a fantastic school and it will suit you. So I applied, and was invited to a formal interview with the Headmaster.

As it turned out, the Head and I met by chance on the previous evening. I had been looking around the school and, on the spur of the moment, decided to go for a quick drink in the small staff bar. There was only one other person there, a total stranger, and I thought I would be friendly.

"Hello, my name is Floyd," I said, while ordering an Irish whiskey. "Would you let me get you one of these as well?"

The total stranger turned out to be Michael Caulfield, founding headmaster of the school. We chatted, and he said he wanted to encourage rugby. I told him about my involvement in the game. As we spoke, and ordered a couple more Irish whiskeys, I sensed the interview would go well.

Sure enough, I was offered the position of 'Head of Boys Games' at the co-educational Bishop Douglass Catholic School, and began to encourage more students to play rugby in winter, and also cricket in summer.

It was an excellent school with a strong identity. Around 1,100 students were divided into six houses, each named after a Christian martyr, canonised by the Catholic Church, and each with its own colour which members of that house would wear on their school uniform. Such details may seem insignificant, but, in my experience, they encourage a sense of belonging.

As teachers, we were encouraged to take the students into London, to show them interesting places and new experiences.

On one occasion, I took my form of 16-year-olds to have dinner at a restaurant in Chinatown, just south of Soho. Everything went well until, without warning, an argument broke out in the kitchen and three of the chefs stormed into the restaurant, threatening each other with cleavers.

For a few scary moments, we felt like extras in a horror movie. I instructed the students to take cover under the tables, but the chaos passed, and we all got home safe and sound, with a story to tell.

Our local MP was Margaret Thatcher, Prime Minister. She had been the Member of Parliament for Finchley since 1959. In December 1987, a few months after winning the third of her three General

Election victories, she visited our school to open a brand new fitness centre. My wife Denise and I generally stood to the left of centre on the political spectrum, but there was no doubt about Mrs Thatcher's sense of presence, and I enjoyed spending time with her.

A report appeared in the local newspaper, which read: "Bishop Douglass School students flexed their muscles for the Prime Minister when she officially opened the £100,000 fitness centre there on Friday. Lower sixth student, Bill Fenoughty (16), of Mill Hill, showed the PM how the high pulley machine helped work the stomach muscles. Under the direction of PE teacher Floyd Steadman, the teenager demonstrated his prowess on the machine before he was stopped by the PM, who clearly felt he was worn out. The student insisted he could have stayed on the machine far longer."

We were not exactly hitting global headlines, but it was exciting at the time. In fairness, Mrs Thatcher was an effective constituency MP, who made her presence felt in our part of London.

Another time, I took the Saracens squad to dinner at a restaurant run by the parents of a girl at Bishop Douglass. I wanted to support the owners, who had been eager to show me, in pride of place on the wall, a framed letter from their famous local MP, saying how much she liked their restaurant.

Everything went well until, the next day, I received a telephone call from the restaurant owners, telling me 'Mrs Thatcher's letter has disappeared'. I read the riot act to the players at Saracens training that evening, and asked for the letter to be returned. The unknown prankster obliged, thankfully.

Bishop Douglass was a fine school, and the overwhelming majority of students were thriving. However there are vulnerable children in each and every school and, perhaps because of my own experiences, I have always tried to keep an eye out for the pupils most in need.

I remember one 16-year-old Irish girl, who was suffering from some form of addiction. Her father didn't trust the high street banks and preferred to keep his savings in a bag under his mattress. In any event, this particular girl had taken the money and run away; she became the object of a frantic search by her parents, the police and social services.

They asked if I would help. I did a bit of digging around and managed to make contact with the girl via some of her friends. We arranged to meet in a cafe. If she was feeling 'excited and terrified' all at once, then I knew how she felt. I explained that everybody wanted to help her and that nobody was angry with her, and I persuaded her to go back to her parents. They welcomed her home and, so far as I know, the outcome for this young person was much better than it had been for another runaway 15 years earlier.

I worked at Bishop Douglass Catholic School for five years, and was extremely happy, at least until the school announced plans to merge the two positions of Head of Boys Games and Head of Girls Games into one more senior role. I was excited and I applied for the new job, only to be told it was unlikely I would be promoted because I was not a practising Catholic.

Disappointment can throw you off course. Sometimes, when things don't go as you had hoped, the best option is actually to do nothing, to sit back and wait for as long as it takes for the waves of emotion to subside, and only then to assess the situation and decide the best way forward.

When my path was blocked at Bishop Douglass, disenchanted, I opted to step away from education and try something else.

"Come on, Floyd, rugby is getting more commercial. The game is going to turn professional some time soon. We've started a company to create commercial opportunities for the players, appearances at lunches, that kind of thing. With your connections, this would suit you well."

"I'm really not sure."

"Come on, Floyd, you may as well give it a go."

Simon Carter, then president of Camberley RFC, and his business partner Mal Malik, a mover and shaker at Rugby RFC, were imploring me to join their marketing and promotions company, Prisma.

"You will fit in very well, Floyd," Simon said. "Alex Keay has already joined us, and you know how well you work with him."

Maybe, for once, it was time to take a detour from the straight road. Simon was right. I may as well give it a go. So I resigned at Bishop Douglass at the end of the summer term, and stepped into a brave new world.

Rugby was still supposed to be an amateur sport, but various under-the-table payments were becoming more common. Leading players noticed the growing revenue being generated from sponsors, broadcasters and gate receipts, and began to wonder if they should be sharing the dividends.

Prisma planned to operate on the margin of the regulations. We were going to organise a wide range of events, which made money for top players, and for us.

"Right, Floyd, we're organising a Sportsman's lunch in November, when the All Blacks are here," I was told. "We need you to get a few well-known sportsmen in the room, and, between us, here's a kitty of £2,000."

"No problem," I replied.

Within a couple of weeks, I had secured commitments to attend our lunch from a well-known New Zealand loose forward, for £500, from a celebrated Scotland back, for another £500, and from a couple of England Test cricketers, an Olympic athlete and a world champion boxer, all for £200 each. My boss was happy with my work.

The New Zealander was also pleased, so much so that he asked us to create more discreet opportunities for him during the tour. We worked hard, and helped him earn an extra £10,000.

The model seemed to work. We became successful, in fact too successful for our own good. The Rugby Football Union took steps abruptly to close down Prisma, and we were all made redundant. We had been six or seven years ahead of our time.

I had no job. Alex Keay had no job. What now? Alex said why don't he and I start our own business, doing roughly the same thing as Prisma but without attracting the ire of the RFU. I liked the idea, and I liked Alex, and this seemed like a sensible way forward.

It's strange how life works, how something can just happen without warning, and, all of a sudden, you move in a different direction.

John Atkin, a friend from Borough Road College who played rugby at Quins, telephoned me out of the blue, and told me how he had been working at Colet Court school, how he had recently been promoted, how the Headmaster had asked if he could think of anybody to take his old job.

"And I said you would be ideal," he said. "They really want to meet you."

"Colet Court?" I asked. "Isn't that the prep school for St Paul's?"

"Exactly," John said.

A lunch was arranged for me to meet Canon Peter Pilkington, high master of St Paul's School, and Billy Howard, headmaster of Colet Court, and, as I recall, at the exact moment that the decanter of port was passed in my direction, I was offered the full-time position as Head of Sport at the prep school. I called Alex that evening, apologised and said I would go back to teaching. I hate letting anybody down, but he understood and wished me well.

St Paul's School was ranked among the finest independent schools in England, a member of the educational Premier League. Founded by John Colet in 1509, early in the reign of King Henry VIII, it was originally located in the grounds of St Paul's Cathedral but moved to the current site at Barnes, 43 acres on the south side of a bend in the River Thames, in 1968.

The prep school opened in 1881, offering education from the age of seven to 14, providing an ideal preparation for St Paul's. For the next 109 years, it so happened that Colet Court appointed white teachers, and more white teachers until, in September 1990, I became the first black man to be employed as a teacher at the school.

I had agreed to teach at a private school, where parents were paying tens of thousands of pounds for their children to be educated. Having only worked at state schools, I guessed an adjustment would be required on all sides.

"Excuse me, would you direct me to the staff room?"

"Sorry?"

It was my first day at Colet Court, and the question seemed simple enough.

"The staff room, please," I repeated. "Could you direct me to the staff room?"

"Oh, sorry, you mean the Common Room. It's over there."

I would have to learn a new language. I eventually found my way to the room designated for staff, known as the Common Room, where I settled into one of several well-worn and extremely comfortable leather sofas.

"Er, I wouldn't sit there," ventured one of my new colleagues, gently, genuinely trying to help. "One of the senior teachers has sat in that place on that sofa for the past 17 years, and it has sort of become his place now."

I thanked him for the heads-up, gathered my books and moved to a different sofa, hoping I had found a vacant spot.

Adjustment was indeed going to be required on all sides.

At my first staff meeting, one of the senior masters referred to someone called 'Black Rose'. I was surprised. He mentioned 'Black Rose' again, and I wondered who he was talking about. Afterwards, I asked. "Oh, yes," he explained. "Black Rose is an African woman, who works in the kitchen."

I felt uncomfortable. I explained my concerns to the master, without hysterics or argument, quietly. He never used the name 'Black Rose' again. I am sure he meant no offence, and the nickname had probably been used for years, but it was still wrong and I had felt obliged to say so. I didn't want to cause trouble, and I didn't want to be seen as any kind of rebel but, if it was possible to make a positive impact, then I was eager to do so.

Colet Court, renamed St Paul's Juniors in September 2016, was an exceptional school in many respects; in the sports department, we were able to attract highly talented young sports people and to offer a range of sporting facilities, which would have made a medium-sized town proud. The combination created exciting opportunities, and I loved the work.

We had assembled an impressive team in the PE department, which included the likes of Les Barlow, Tony Lewis and Glen Harrison.

Les had been an England and Lions reserve during his playing days at Rosslyn Park, and we had to got to know each other well when, for a few weeks during school holidays in 1985, we were both invited to travel to Canada and coach at Leftbridge RFC, in Alberta.

Tony was a talented and enthusiastic Kiwi, who started at the same time as me and has since navigated a successful career in sport, recently being appointed as CEO of the Western Force franchise in Perth, Australia. Glen was also a highly effective coach, who worked at Colet Court at the same time as he fulfilled the role of Will Carling's understudy in the Quins midfield.

In December 1990, we hosted a touring rugby side from one of the major private schools in Australia. After the match, we were invited to make the return trip. I sensed some of my colleagues were hesitating. I was told the school rarely embarked on such overseas tours. Well why not, I asked?

During my 11 years working at Colet Court, I helped to organise that return rugby tour to Australia in 1992, a rugby tour to South Africa, a football tour to Miami, another football tour to Boston and a skiing trip to Whistler Mountain, in British Columbia, Canada, the largest ski resort in North America. I had experienced all the significant benefits of touring as a rugby player, and I was very happy to create similar experiences for the students.

The 1999 tour to South Africa was memorable. We raised funds by arranging for Richard Attenborough, the filmmaker whose grandson was in the school, to host a private screening of his film 'Cry Freedom', the epic drama released in 1987 which told the stories of Steve Biko, the South African black activist, and his friend Donald Woods, a newspaper editor.

I stood to one side, and listened to the fascinating hour of questions and answers that followed... and almost felt the urge to pinch myself, just to make sure it was really happening. Mixing in such circles felt a long way from the children's home.

We played the junior teams of some of South Africa's leading schools, including Bishops and SACS High School in Cape Town and Paarl Boys High in Paarl, and we also played against Clifton Prep School on the famous first team field at Hilton College in Pietermaritzburg.

The rugby was tough, especially in Paarl where the home side chose to play barefoot, and our boys were obliged to do the same. In fact, that particular match turned out to be the only defeat on what was a hugely successful tour.

After the match in Paarl, the headmaster asked me if I would be prepared to speak to his entire school at assembly the next morning. South Africa was changing at speed, Nelson Mandela had just stepped down after one term as President, to be succeeded by Thabo Mbeki, and I was pleased to share my thoughts with a hall full of mostly white South African schoolboys.

Our tour squad also participated in outreach programmes in South Africa. Around £50,000 had been raised before we left home, and this money was spent on the provision of educational equipment to two schools, Nomzamzo School in Somerset West and Combined School in Nottingham Road. We visited both.

The boys are in their thirties now, but I still hear from a few of them and they still talk about our tour to South Africa in 1999.

Year on year, the students came and the students went. This is the reality for every teacher: you help young people along, but they are always moving and, in what seems the blink of an eye, they move away. There was the son of David Mellor, QC, who was a member of John Major's Cabinet between 1990 and 1992. There was the son of David and Elizabeth Emanuel, who had designed the wedding dress worn by Diana, Princess of Wales, in 1981.

There was Dan Snow, son of Peter Snow, the broadcaster and master of the BBC 'swingometer' on General Election nights. Dan is now a well-known historian and broadcaster in his own right.

And there was an obviously extremely talented young actor and singer who arrived from Eaton House, shone at Colet Court and then left to go to Eton... his name was Eddie Redmayne.

After seven years as Head of Sport, and geography teacher and form tutor, I saw the position of Deputy Headmaster at Colet Court became vacant and applied. It felt like my dream job at a world class school, but this dream did not come true. I was overlooked and a younger candidate, ostensibly with less experience, was offered the job. I was extremely disappointed.

Perhaps sensing my dismay, the school promoted me to the senior leadership team and I was given an expanded role as 'Head of Juniors', which included pastoral responsibility for 250 of the younger boys. I was gaining knowledge and experience, but the job felt like a consolation prize.

I stayed at the school for another four years, but eventually accepted that I was facing a simple choice: either stay at Colet Court, or move to another school and pursue my ambition to become a headmaster.

I didn't want to leave. I enjoyed the school, the students and parents, and I would happily have stayed for the remainder of my career; in fact, several of my colleagues from the 1990s are still working there. I was pleased when I was made an honorary old boy, an Old Pauline, after more than ten years' service, and I remain exceptionally proud to be associated with the school.

However, I sorely wanted to be a headmaster. I wanted to prove, to myself and to everyone else that, even if I had not come from much, I had the ability and the capacity to run a school. I had reached the stage where I wanted to be promoted, not just employed.

# Chapter 9

# **Promoted**

There is an expression, a look of uncertainty, a quizzical eye, a raised eyebrow, even a forced smile. The message is unspoken but unmistakable. Are you sure you're in the right place? Has there been some mistake?

Maybe it would have been easier if my surname was Tshabalala or any name which more clearly indicated the colour of my skin. The issue with the name 'Floyd Steadman' is that it almost sounds as if I could be white.

After so many happy and successful years working at Colet Court Preparatory School, I absolutely believed I was ready to become an effective headmaster. I offered the skills, the track record and the experience, and was applying for suitable vacancies across the region. My preference was to make one single leap to become a headmaster. However, if necessary, I was prepared to move forward in two steps and first become a deputy head.

My application was almost always well received and, usually, I would be placed on a short list and be invited to an interview. I went through a similar process once, then again and again. A pattern evolved.

"Good morning," I say. "I am here for the interviews."

"Oh yes," replies the receptionist. "Which interviews?"

"The interviews for the position of headmaster," I say.

A look of uncertainty follows, a quizzical eye, a raised eyebrow.

"Oh yes, and your name please?"

"Floyd Steadman."

"Oh yes, of course," she says, with an ostensibly forced smile. "I can see your name now. Please take a seat, and someone will be with you shortly."

So I sit and wait patiently, dressed in jacket and tie, ready and prepared to explain how I believe I will be able to provide leadership and direction to the school. After a few minutes, somebody appears and I am led into a room where the interview panel is sitting on the opposite side of the table. Usually there are as many as six members. Usually they are school governors. Usually they are older than 60, often a lot older. Usually they are white. Usually, they are cautious and conservative, often with capital 'C's.

"Ah, Mr Steadman, thank you for coming in today," says the main man, sitting in the middle, his blazer buttoned, working hard to put me at ease. "Would you perhaps start by explaining your general philosophy?"

"Of course," I say, smiling, working hard to appear confident, to convince them that, notwithstanding appearances, I belong in the same place. "I believe there are three key elements in my approach to running a school.

"The first is 'provide strong leadership'. The head must get to know the school, where it fits, what it does well and what it needs to improve. This knowledge leads to the development of a clear, integrated strategy, and it is the head's task to be a strong leader, who communicates and drives that plan. If running the school can be likened to driving a car, the head must be seen to be in the driver's seat with both hands firmly on the steering wheel, not reclining on the back seat, gazing out the window and enjoying the view.

"The second is 'educate the whole student'. Achieving the strongest possible academic performance is important, and so is music, sport, public speaking and much else. Our great task is to search for the strength of each and every pupil – and each and every pupil does have a strength – and then to nurture and enhance that strength because that will build confidence and encourage growth and development in other areas.

"The third is 'act with compassion always'. We are mentors as well as teachers, and we need to be relentlessly positive role models who offer pastoral care in everything we say and do. We never shout or threaten or seek to intimidate in any way. Discipline is obviously important but, as my mentor Derek Rosenberg taught me, we should punish the act, not the pupil."

The panel appear to be listening intently.

The main man speaks again. "That's an interesting concept, Mr Steadman," he says. "When you speak of punishing the act and not the pupil, you must surely recognise there will always be a few students who are disruptive and who need to be disciplined."

"Of course," I reply. "The head should not hesitate to be strict when required, but it's possible to be strict with care and compassion. At one of my previous schools, there was one particular boy of dual heritage who many of the teachers seemed to regard as disruptive. He was getting a lot of things wrong, but labelling him as difficult and punishing him over and over again was not improving the situation. In my view, we had fallen into the trap of punishing the student, instead of the act, and getting nowhere.

"So we took an active decision to wipe the slate clean and to start making him feel supported. He was still punished if he did anything wrong, but we worked hard to ensure he felt fundamentally liked and respected, and the results were outstanding. He began to make excellent progress."

"Thank you, Mr Steadman," says the main man, and he looks around at his colleagues, inviting them to ask any questions.

"Thank you," says another member of the panel. "Mr Steadman, could you tell us a little more about your personal qualities?"

"Certainly," I reply. "I believe I have a particular ability to connect with people, whether it is students, parents or my colleagues. I try to be calm and treat everybody with respect. I have no problem with being firm when required, but I try to approach every individual and situation with a resolve to make things better; and people generally seem to respond well, and the outcome is usually positive."

"Thank you, Mr Steadman."

A few more questions follow, and I provide more answers, and the interview seems to go extremely well, and I smile and thank them for their time and they say they will contact me shortly. As the pattern continues, I would receive a letter a week or so later, saying they have offered the position to someone else.

This process, or something very similar, unfolded once, twice, five times, ten times, maybe even 15 times over what became an intensely frustrating period, leading me to reach the conclusion that, even if I was qualified to be a headmaster, panel after panel was reluctant to appoint a black man to lead their school.

For panel after panel, it seemed safer to appoint a white candidate, even if he or she had less experience.

That seemed to be the reality. Maybe you should just accept the fact, I told myself, that you will never be a headmaster in England. There had been offers to take senior leadership roles at schools in Australia and South Africa but, as a family, we were settled in London and did not want to move abroad.

As ever, there was no point in protesting, and there were no hysterics and no arguments, but I was not ready to accept this situation. I would be persistent, and would keep applying again and again and again. I would keep banging my head against what felt like a glass ceiling, until it broke into a thousand pieces and I was given a chance to lead a school in England.

Why didn't you protest, people have asked me. I saw no point in raging against being overlooked because I would have been dismissed as just somebody with a chip on his shoulder. I decided I would simply keep applying, keep attending interviews, keep pounding the stone until it shattered.

My experiences in rugby were helpful. I had over the years grown accustomed to being picked for representative teams only if I could prove myself much better – not just better but much better – than my rivals. The same challenge applied in my quest to become a headmaster. So be it.

Another day dawned, in the spring of 2001, bringing another telephone call and another bend in the winding road of my career.

"Hi, Floyd," he said. "It's Kevin Douglas here. How are you?"

Kevin was a wonderfully skilful loose forward at Saracens in the early 1980s, and had in fact been my vice-captain in 1982. He was a teacher as well, and he told me he had been offered a new job as Headmaster at University College Junior School (UCS) in

Hampstead, and was going to resign as Deputy Head at Belmont Prep, the junior school to Mill Hill School in north London.

"I wanted to let you know, Floyd, because I really think you should apply for the vacancy at Belmont. It will suit you really well."

"Thanks, Kevin," I said, preparing to start the process all over again.

On this occasion, however, the process had an unexpected end. I was offered the position and, after leaving Colet Court with a heavy heart, started my new job as Deputy Headmaster of the co-educational Belmont Preparatory School in September 2001. I happily settled into a new routine of working as a manager in the mornings, teaching in the afternoons and then attending to some more managerial and strategic issues in the evening.

At last, I was making real progress.

Several well-known Arsenal and Tottenham Hotspur footballers chose to send their children to Belmont, and they provided some interesting moments on the touchline at school matches.

There always seemed to be significantly more mothers watching whenever David Ginola, the French international, was present, and I recall Jens Lehmann, the German goalkeeper and member of the Arsenal 'Invincibles' side of 2003/2004, watching his son, Mats, play rugby. "I know absolutely nothing about this game," he told me, "but I am a big supporter."

Certainly one of the most memorable requests for time away from school was made by one particular girl in June 2002, when she asked for a week off so she could fly to Tokyo and 'watch my dad play in the World Cup final'. In the event, her father, Christian Ziege, the Tottenham and Germany defender, came on as an 84th-minute substitute in the 2-0 defeat against Brazil.

Another day dawned, in the summer of 2005, bringing another telephone call and another bend in the winding road of my career.

"Hello, Floyd," he said. "This is Chris Woodhead speaking."

I recognised the name. Chris had worked as Her Majesty's Chief Inspector of Schools in England from 1994 until 2000, and, as head of OFSTED, the Office for Standards in Education, controversially advocated traditional teaching as preferable to various 'trendy' theories. When he said he was paid to challenge "mediocrity, failure and complacency", he was heavily criticised by the teaching unions and many in the profession.

For my part, I liked him and generally empathised with his views. He resigned from OFSTED in November 2000 and subsequently founded Cognita, a company that would grow to own and run 85 independent schools throughout the world, in the United Kingdom, Hong Kong, Singapore, Spain, Brazil, Vietnam, Switzerland, Thailand, India, Chile and the UAE.

With Chris serving as chairman, Cognita operated its first school at Quinton House School, Northampton in 2004 and then acquired the Asquith Court group of 18 schools.

"Hello, Chris," I replied, wondering why he was calling.

"Floyd, we need people like you," he said. "We are acquiring private schools around the world and we need people with your kind of experience, character and skills to provide direction and strong leadership. Would you be interested?"

I carefully considered his enquiry, weighing up all the pros and cons for a few seconds, and then responded: "Absolutely, yes."

We arranged to have lunch in Milton Keynes and, soon afterwards, Chris asked me to become Headmaster of Salcombe Preparatory

School, an independent school for girls and boys aged between three and 11, located on two neighbouring sites in Southgate, literally two minutes walk from Bramley Road. It appeared to be an ideal opportunity in happily familiar surroundings.

I started at Salcombe Prep in January 2006 and, soon after my arrival, I recall going for a walk around the school, greeting students and staff, being visible as the new headmaster, getting a feel for the place. There were a few 11-year-old boys playing football, and one of the group made an immediate impression on me: he was tall, wonderfully athletic, talented and black.

"Hello," I said, "I'm Mr Steadman, the new headmaster."

The youngster smiled back and said: "Hello, sir."

"Have you ever thought about playing rugby," I asked, almost casually, just as an aside. "You could enjoy that particular game."

"Rugby? No, sir, I have never played rugby," he said.

"You really should try it," I said, as I continued my stroll.

That particular youngster was midway though his final year at Salcombe and, five months later, he moved on to St George's School in Harpenden, where he was offered the chance to play rugby. He eagerly embraced the game, and won a scholarship to Harrow School, where he took his A levels.

He did indeed start to enjoy rugby, playing for junior sides at Harpenden RFC and then for a year at Old Albanian RFC in St Albans, before being asked to join the Saracens Academy and signing his first professional contract in 2012, at the age of 18. He made his debut for Saracens in an LV Cup match against Cardiff in January 2013, in what was the club's first ever competitive match at their new home stadium, Allianz Park, in Barnet.

Maro Itoje has since advanced to be one of the most admired players in world rugby, a wonderfully athletic and talented forward, equally effective in the back row and the second row, a key performer for Saracens, for England and indeed for the British and Irish Lions as well. Beyond all this, he remains an intelligent and balanced young man, admirable in so many ways.

At the end of one particular England tour, the 3-0 series victory in Australia in 2016, when his son had excelled on the field, Efe Itoje, Maro's father, was kind enough to make contact with me and thanked me for encouraging his son to start playing rugby.

I worked at Salcombe Prep for two and half years before Chris Woodhead and Jim Hudson, Chief Education Officer at Cognita, asked me to move again and apply for the position of Headmaster at Downsend School in Leatherhead, located in the affluent and leafy suburbs of Surrey. It was a large job at a large school, with 850 students on four different sites.

One glance at the map made me hesitate. My daily routine would be an hour and 20 minutes in the car driving from our family home in Hanwell to Downsend early in the morning, 10 or 11 hours working at the school and then another hour and 20 minutes driving home at night. I was going to become very well acquainted with the M25, the motorway around London, although it would be an exaggeration to say we would ever become friends.

Chris and Jim had just asked me to apply, explaining the appointment would only be made after a thorough process, which involved parents. I agreed and entered a gruelling series of interviews. A few weeks later, my appointment as the new headmaster of Downsend was confirmed.

"Excuse me, Mr Steadman, could we speak to you please," asked a member of a group of parents, a few weeks after my arrival.

"Of course," I said. "How can I help?"

A clearly distressed and embarrassed woman, with two children in the school, said: "We wanted to tell you we are aware of some parents, who have made it clear they do not support the appointment of a black headmaster, and we want to let you know that you have our full support."

"Let's not worry about that," I told her. "That's not our problem. I am going to be headmaster of this school, and I will work to the best of my ability. Let's focus on the work that lies ahead."

Once again, others were more concerned by conscious racism than me. Just as Alex Keay, the Saracens captain, had been more bothered when opposing forwards were making racial remarks 20 years earlier, so these parents were much more disturbed than me by the racist views of others.

So far as I was concerned, sporadic conscious racism was a fact of life. It was their problem, not my problem.

I spent five years at Downsend, a fantastic school with a fantastic culture, and felt proud to be leading an organisation with few students and staff of colour. I was black, the vast majority of them were white. It didn't matter. We worked successfully towards one clearly defined goal... giving each of the constituent parts of the school a much greater degree of autonomy, while ensuring each and every department – pre-prep schools, prep etc. – adopted and maintained the same core principles of excellence and compassion.

The effective implementation of this strategy helped transform the school from being perceived as a somewhat reluctant member of the group into what many increasingly regarded as the flagship, embodying what became known as 'The Cognita Way'. Our vision statement included six elements which we felt were required in successful schools: energised leadership, personalised learning, people growth, community, innovation and brilliant basics.

These are fine words but, at Downsend and elsewhere, they were transferred into actions, which delivered an excellent education.

Downsend thrived, and continues to thrive under the excellent leadership of Ian Thorpe, who succeeded me as headmaster.

In 2013, realising the demanding daily commute was not sustainable, I suggested to Cognita that it was necessary for me to step down, and spend more time at home with my wife and three sons, who were beginning an important phase of their lives, sitting exams, and deserved to see more of their father.

"We understand, Floyd," said Ed Hyslop, the Chief Executive (Europe) at Cognita, "but we don't want to lose you, so we will find a school closer to your home."

In some ways, I was becoming regarded as a 'Cognita fixer', a headmaster who would be introduced to a school where a specific issue had been identified and a specific plan needed to be implemented. This role meant I would rarely stay at a school for longer than, say, four or five years, which was often hard for me because I would become attached, very attached, to staff, students and parents, and would then have to move on. On the other hand, I enjoyed the challenge of change management, of developing a clear strategy, of winning hearts and minds and then executing the plan.

For me, each appointment as headmaster was a journey, with a clear start, a set roadmap to follow and, in most cases, a clear end.

My next destination was Clifton Lodge School, a small, friendly co-educational preparatory school and nursery in Ealing, across the road from the entrance to Walpole Park, less than two miles from our home.

It was my third appointment and I was gaining in confidence, learning from my experiences at Salcombe and Downsend. Every head teacher needs to exude a sense of purpose and self-assurance when, in reality, we are just as anxious to succeed and as vulnerable as anybody else.

There were specific challenges at Clifton Lodge, and hard decisions had to be taken, but we made progress and the school was soon delivering both a strong academic performance and 'wrap-around' care from 8am to 6pm. We found a clear sense of purpose, and began to play an increasingly important role within what was a diverse and dynamic part of west London.

Three years passed until, in 2016, the planners at Cognita worked out my son Josh was reaching an age where he would be going off to university, and I was asked whether it might be feasible for me to accept a new challenge at a new school a little further afield.

I tapped a new name into my car's satellite navigation system... Cumnor House School, 168 Pampisford Road, South Croydon, CR2 6DA. The computer showed a 52-minute drive through Hammersmith, Wandsworth and Streatham into the depths of south London. All right, I decided, it's doable.

Cumnor House is a group of schools, offering girls and boys aged two to 13 a journey which starts at one of two co-educational nurseries, in either Purley and South Croydon, and transitions to one of two single sex Preparatory Schools, Cumnor House School for Boys or Cumnor House School for Girls.

A high quality all-round education is provided, although the school is renowned for the quality of its sport, and is proud of old boys such as Chris Robshaw, the Harlequins and England rugby captain, Mark Butcher and Alistair Brown, who both played cricket for Surrey and England and, most recently, Elliot Daly, who excels for Saracens, England and the British Lions.

The challenge was to streamline the systems and structure of this significant organisation. It was an interesting and complex task but, unfortunately, I was never able to get a real grip on the job. Only a week after I arrived as the new headmaster, my wife was diagnosed with breast cancer and, as her illness took its course, it became increasingly hard for me to provide the support which she needed, and the commitment which the school required.

Cognita remained wonderfully supportive through these difficult days, and it was eventually agreed that I would return to Clifton Lodge in Ealing, and work as Executive Head on a part-time basis. The specific challenge was to integrate two new colleagues into an effective senior management team, and I greatly enjoyed working with some special people: Beth Friel was the Head of School, Camille Hickmot was Deputy Head, Dorothy Trill served as Business Manager, and Sue Ward was both the Bursar and Marketing Manager. In fact, everything went so well, I started calling us the 'Dream Team'.

I continued working at Clifton Lodge through the 2019/20 academic year, and was involved in guiding the school through the start of the Covid-19 pandemic, until, in March 2020, I stepped down and retired.

My teacher career unfolded over a period of 39 years, led me through eight schools, each with their own strengths, and gave me the opportunity to work as headmaster of four schools. I was honoured to strive alongside so many wonderful staff, privileged to teach so many talented students and pleased to engage with so many interesting and supportive parents.

Schools are special places, communities within communities. They are places where you need to expect the unexpected, where new challenges arise every single day... they are places where, at their best, everyone is focused on the clear goal of giving the children a brilliant start in life.

I look back on these four decades of teaching with a sense of pride that, against the odds, I was able to achieve my goal of becoming a headmaster.

It is my greatest hope that I was able to make a positive impact on each of these eight schools and that, more specifically, in homes and businesses across the country, there are individuals who will feel pleased Mr Steadman played a role in their education.

I hope I proved deserving of the trust placed in me by Cognita and by so many parents, and that I was worthy of being promoted.

# Chapter 10

# Loved

We met in September 1977 during our first week as students at Borough Road College, and something seemed to click. She was bright, fun and beautiful. She was calm, intelligent and sympathetic. She was perfect. In fact, for almost four decades, Denise would be the one true love of my life.

I was always busy, of course... busy with studies, busy with rugby, busy with teaching, busy just trying to get by and survive, but she always seemed to be there, an ever-present source of encouragement and love.

We mixed in the same circle of friends at first, casually, without pressure, just two members of a loose group gathered at college from different backgrounds, socialising, going to parties, enjoying nights out now and then.

There were the boys: Andy Phillips, who would be my teammate at Saracens and best man, Steve French, who emigrated to Australia, Paul Cochrane, Nigel Rees, who would play for London Welsh, and Colin Coombs-Goodfellow, from Jersey, and me. There were the girls: Jane Ovenden, whose uncle was Tony Bodley, the rugby correspondent of the Daily Express, Katrina Knight, Sophie Karsa, Wendy Tremineer and Denise Friggens.

This group generally stuck together during the first year, and then through the second year. Most of the boys were sportsmen and most of the girls were more academic, but we got along, and laughed, and laughed.

"Friggen' hell, Denise, what do you think you are doing?" We used to tease her about her unusual surname, and she would smile.

Perhaps there was safety in numbers. Perhaps there was security in the group, with nothing too intense and no fear of rejection. Perhaps I was too focused on my studies and my rugby, and didn't have time to invest in any kind of serious relationship. For whatever reason, although I really liked her from the first day we met, it was some time before I asked her out.

"Er, Denise, I was wondering if you might like to go to see a film?"

"Sure, Floyd, that sounds like fun."

So, we would go to a film together, and then there would be rugby on the next few weekends, and we wouldn't see each other for a while. And then I would suggest we go somewhere else together, and she would agree, and we would have a good time. Into the third year at Borough Road, we were never far from each other, but we were on, and off, then on and then off.

"So, Floyd, I was wondering..."

"Yes, Denise?"

"I was wondering if you are free over New Year, and whether you might like to come and spend a few days with me and my family in Cornwall."

"Of course," I replied immediately.

This invitation felt like a major step forward for both of us. It was the last few days of 1979. I was black. She was white. We did like each other, a lot, but we both knew a relationship was going to be complicated.

The trip was arranged, and I travelled by train from Paddington, in London, to Penzance. Everything was new to me. I remember arriving at the station, looking around and quickly realising that, in this south-west corner of England, there were not many people who looked anything like me. In fact, there were no people who looked anything like me. Never mind, I thought, if it was all new for me, then it would also be a new experience for them.

Denise had given me detailed directions and, from Penzance railway station, I managed to catch the correct bus, which took me around 15 minutes, up a steep hill, into Madron. All was quiet, and the view towards the east, across the bay towards St Michael's Mount, was spectacular.

The next challenge was to find the home of Denise's family. As I checked her instructions again, I noticed a net curtain twitch in the front window of a small terraced house across the road. I looked up, and saw nothing, but knew someone had seen me. Moments later, a mother and her young child walked past, and the boy stared, and stared, and stared at me. I found the house and, feeling a little nervous, knocked on the front door.

"Hello," said Denise, beaming. "You made it!"

From that moment until today, and hopefully for as long as I live, I have been made to feel extraordinarily welcome by the entire Friggens family. It has been one of the great pleasures of my life to be accepted as one of their own, to be made to feel at home and to be unconditionally loved.

"This is my mother Joan and this is my father Dennis," said Denise, introducing me to her parents. "I have seven sisters and three brothers, so maybe you can meet some of them a little later, once you have settled."

We stayed at home that evening and I learned how, like me, Denise had always wanted to become a teacher, and had initially planned to study in Aberystwyth, but that had not materialised and she entered the clearing process, which brought the offer of a place at Borough Road College. London is a long way from Cornwall, but she embraced the challenge.

There are two major families in Madron, they explained, the Friggens and the Nichols. It was not exactly medieval Italy, but Dennis was a Friggens and Joan was a Nichols, so their marriage might be said to have united the parish, in some ways. Dennis worked as a carpenter and a foreman, and Joan looked after the children. The more they spoke, the more I listened and admired the love which bound their family together. I had never experienced this sense of being a unit and being together through good times and bad.

On New Year's Eve, Denise, her parents and I went to a party hosted by her brother, Randal. Everyone seemed happy to see each other. Everyone seemed to be talking at once. Everyone seemed to be laughing. I had never seen such a large family gathered together, celebrating together.

"Right," said Denise, as midnight approached, and the new year celebrations started to move up a gear, "it's time for some introductions."

Raising her voice, she proclaimed: "Everyone, this is Floyd."

"Now, Floyd, you'll have to concentrate," she continued. "The oldest is my brother Randal, and then it's John, then Angela and then Liz. They're the four oldest: Randal, John, Angela and Liz. Have you got that?"

I nodded, smiling, trying to remember everything.

Denise went on: "Caroline is next, then Jeff and, number seven, that's me. You have that, Floyd? That's the first seven, and then there are four more sisters, which makes eleven. It's easy to remember. The first two of the last four are twins, Sally and Sue, followed by Mandy and Janet. That's everyone. OK, now you have to try and tell me everyone's name."

The happiest of New Year celebrations continued with a lunch-time drink the following day, even if it was slightly unnerving for me to walk into the pub full of people and to see every person in that pub stop talking, turn and look directly at me, in silence. You would have thought some of them had never seen a black man in their life. In reality, some of them probably hadn't.

There was a television commercial for Strongbow cider in the 1980s, in which a bustling pub suddenly falls silent when a smart couple, dressed in black tie and white fur, walk through the door. They approach the bar, and the man orders a 'Daiquiri for the lady' before asking nervously 'what do people order around here'. It's only when he orders himself 'a pint of Strongbow' that everybody in the pub relaxes, approves and resumes their conversation.

Well, after my first pub visit in Madron, I understood how the man in the TV ad might have felt. The first few minutes were a little tense, but we sensed the locals were curious, rather than racist. It wasn't long before everyone relaxed, and we enjoyed our drinks in friendly surroundings.

A couple of years later Denise and I, and two of our friends, Bob and Mandy Simons, arrived at a pub in Newlyn, near Penzance; as we walked in to the main bar, somebody shouted out: "Oh, my God, look who's here. It's Lenny Henry!"

I instinctively turned around to look for the popular actor, singer, comedian and television presenter, star of The Lenny Henry Show, to see if I could see where he was sitting. He was nowhere to be seen. It was only then that I realised the local man was in fact referring to me because I was black.

To their credit, Bob and Mandy were furious but Denise and I urged them to ignore the remark. It was not worth reacting, we said. Let's sit down and not let anything spoil our meal.

Denise and I were seeing each other regularly, but we had to endure some degree of separation in July 1980, when I left college and she stayed for another year at Borough Road to complete her PGCE teaching qualification. Then, a year later, she returned home to Cornwall and taught at St Paul's Junior School in Penzance. Managing a long-distance relationship was not ideal, but we were committed and we made it work.

There were many visits in both directions. When I was in Madron, I would stay either in a single room at the home of Denise's parents or in a single room in the home of Aunt Mary and Uncle Bill. They were close relatives; in truth, they could scarcely have been closer. Mary was a sister of Denise's mother and Bill was a brother of Denise's father. There was never a discussion about whether Denise and I would share a room before we were married. It was not going to happen. Things were done differently in those days.

At last, in January 1983, Denise secured a teaching job at Christ Church Junior School in Ealing, and returned to live in London. I was more certain than ever that we we were meant to be together, and I decided this was the moment to pluck up some courage and to ask the big question.

As ever, I wanted to do things properly, and that meant asking her father for permission to marry his daughter. I explained my intentions to Joan, Denise's mother, who put me somewhat at ease by saying, "I am sure Dennis will say yes, but he will want it done in the right way".

So, with Denise out of the house for some reason, I bought a couple of bottles of champagne and put them in the fridge, and sat in the front room, patiently waiting for Dennis to arrive home from work.

"So, Dennis," I said, "there is something I would like to ask you."

"Yes, Floyd," he said, suddenly seeming extremely solemn.

"Well," I continued, "you know how much I love Denise. I would like your permission to ask her to marry me."

A moment passed.

"Of course, you have my permission," he said, smiling with the depth of sigh that only a father of eight daughters would ever under-stand. "There are just so many weddings. Sally is going to marry Phil later this year. Caroline is getting married to Barry next February and now Denise will be marrying you."

Happily, the financial burden did not fall wholly on Denise's parents. Who paid for yet another wedding? Everyone. What felt like everybody in the village of Madron mucked in and helped us along. Angela, one of Denise's sisters baked the cake, a friend arranged the flowers etc. Such a solution would have been unimaginable in the suburbs of west London, and yet it felt almost natural in west Cornwall, fast becoming a special place for me.

And so, in due course, I asked Denise to marry me, and she said 'yes'. We discussed everything, and planned to set a date in August 1983. We were both 24, quite young by modern standards, but we were excited to start our married life together and we saw no reason for any kind of delay.

For me, the next challenge was to survive my stag party. In fact, there turned out to be three stag parties: one for the four of us physical education teachers sharing a flat in London at the time, one for my teammates at Saracens and then a third for my future brothers-in-law and a few friends in Cornwall.

The third and last event was held in Penzance on the Thursday night, just two days before the wedding, and it involved plenty of alcohol and, as I recall, an impromptu exhibition of some of my finest gymnastics moves. I was relatively fit and agile in those days, and delivered an outstanding performance. One of Denise's older brothers had been allocated the important task of looking after me and ensuring I got home safely. In fact, the roles were reversed, and it was me who took him home and put him to bed.

The sun shone on Saturday 6 August, 1983, both literally and figuratively, and Denise and I were married at St Maddern's Church in the middle of Madron, and the church bells peeled loudly across the parish shortly after three o'clock in the afternoon as Mr and Mrs Floyd Steadman emerged, beaming and blinking into the sunlight, surrounded by their family members.

To be accurate, each of the family members present was related to Denise. None were related to me. I had not known my mother, and I had lost touch with my father and sister. At least, that was true at the start of the day. By the end of the day, after we were married, I felt each and every brother, sister, uncle, aunt and cousin was related as much to me as to Denise. I was so pleased to have married not only a wonderful women, but also into a wonderful family.

We shared so much, not least a passion for rugby. Cornwall was one of the best supported county teams in the country, and there was one great occasion in 1990 when most of the Friggens family joined a boisterous capacity crowd at Redruth to watch Cornwall play a home County Championship semi-final against Middlesex.

I happened to be the captain of Middlesex on this particular afternoon, which meant, I dared hope, there might be at least some slightly divided loyalties. In fact, my wife Denise was interviewed on BBC Radio Cornwall before the match, and she left no doubt who she and her family were supporting, and it wasn't Middlesex.

The game was incredibly physical and finished as a draw, but we went though to the final because we had scored more tries. To judge from the glum expressions on the faces of the Friggens in the bar afterwards, there had certainly been no divided loyalties. For them, it was Cornwall first and last.

That said, two weeks later, on the morning before I played for the Barbarians, I was surprised to receive a telegram, which read: "Best of luck today, love from the Friggens." No question, they are special people.

Madron started to feel like home. It all seemed so unlikely. How had a young black rugby player from the fringes of society in west London ended up feeling so much a part of this village, crowning a hill outside Penzance, so at ease in the King William IV pub, so familiar walking past the terraced houses in Fore Street, so comfortable greeting people and being greeted? I have no idea how it happened, but it did and I will always be grateful.

Denise and I decided we would wait a while before starting a family. We were young teachers, and we wanted to settle down, arrange a mortgage, buy our own flat and get established before the kids came along. We also wanted to spend time together, as a couple, and we went on some wonderful holidays, once to the Florida Keys, twice to The Bahamas, once to Orlando and once for six weeks to South Alberta in Canada, where I played for Leftridge RFC and we had so much fun with our friends, Jan and John Kirman.

We were a dual heritage couple, but we were completely at ease.

There were times when Denise and her sisters would stay out late, and Joan, their mother, would worry until they got home.

"Where have you been," Joan would ask when they arrived back.

"Why were you so worried, Mum," Denise would reply, with a broad grin on her face. "Did you think I had run off with a black man?"

"Please don't talk like that," Joan would say.

"Oh, hold on a minute," Denise would say, as her and her sisters roared with laughter. "I actually did run off with a black man!"

Both of us were at ease, comfortable in our own skins, whether they happened to be white, black or anything in between. Denise could also be strong and confident when required. If somebody ever made any kind of racial remark, she would not hesitate to protest and call out the person who was responsible.

We celebrated the birth of three sons within the space of four and a half-years. Ollie was born in February 1993, Lewis followed in February 1996 and Josh was born in September 1997. All of a sudden, a young couple was transformed into a tight-knit family of five.

These were the happiest of times. More than anything, Denise and I wanted to give our sons as much love and affection as it was possible for parents to give. I recalled what I had craved as a child, and never received; if anything, we may have overcompensated.

152

We did our best, and I think we did a reasonable job, based on the fact that our boys have grown into three decent, confident young black men fiercely proud of their Cornish heritage. We were an effective partnership. There were times when I needed to be firm and Denise would be compassionate, and there were times when she was the 'bad cop', and I would do the comforting.

When the boys were young, we used to spend holidays in Cornwall, staying in a three-bedroom apartment attached to the home of Barry and Caroline, one of Denise's sisters, in Marazion, on the shore of Mount's Bay, a few miles from Madron. There was a wonderful view from the balcony, and we enjoyed many happy times there, just the five of us, together.

The flat worked so well because it meant we had our own base, where we were not in anyone's way, but we were close enough to Madron to be able to see the extended family. Denise's brothers and sisters, would produce, between them, over the years, a total of 21 children, so our boys found themselves constantly enveloped in a doting crowd of uncles, aunts and cousins.

So our lives unfolded with me pursuing my career as a teacher, the boys going to school, playing sport and making friends, and Denise continuing to teach at the same school she had joined in 1983. She had continued to study, and became a expert in Special Educational Needs (SEN), encouraging and supporting some of the most vulnerable children.

Denise was highly respected at work, and the centre of everything at home, as wonderful as a wife and mother as it was possible to be. She had given me the greatest gift.

For almost four decades, she made me feel loved.

# Chapter 11

# Bereaved

It is the news that tens of thousands of people receive every single day of every single year, but it is the news nobody ever expects to hear. For us, the hammer blow was delivered on Friday 26 August, 2016.

"It's not good news," said the doctor, calmly and clearly. "We have found some cancerous cells in your liver and, from what we can tell, this is not the primary tumour. We will have to run some more tests."

"So, I have cancer," said Denise, speaking softly.

"Yes, that's correct," replied the doctor.

In precisely this way, as for so many people, so often, the entire world changes in an instant. Everything that seemed safe and secure suddenly seems fragile. All plans are immediately put on hold, at best.

Denise was everything to me. She was the one true love of my life. She was the source of endless and unconditional love. She was the fountain where my self-confidence and resilience were replenished. Now, sitting beside her in this bland doctor's room, I faced the prospect of losing her.

I remember we drove home together, each of us determined to be strong for the other, each of us trying to understand and accept what we had been told, each of us trying to be practical and work out what needed to be done. We are going to fight this, we agreed. We can beat this together.

You say the words and yet, even as you speak, the fear and the anxiety starts to gnaw at you, somewhere deep inside. No, we're going to be positive. We're going to be fine. Lots of people beat cancer and go on living exactly the kind of blissful, 'normal' life that we were living only yesterday, the day before we got the news. Yes, we believe we can get that life back.

"We can't tell the boys," Denise said. "I don't want to upset them. We can deal with this on our own, Floyd. We definitely can't tell the boys."

I was driving, looking straight ahead, listening to what my wife was saying and completely understanding what she was saying but knowing that, on this issue, she was wrong. Her overriding maternal instinct was to protect her three sons from anything that might hurt them, but she was wrong.

"Denise, I am sorry," I said, speaking slowly, working hard to contain all my emotions. "We have to tell them. They have a right to know."

She said nothing. I knew she agreed. She understood.

The results of the further tests came through several days later, and we were told the cancer had started in her left breast, and had spread not only to her liver but also to her bones. We need to move quickly now, said the doctor, and he prescribed a course of intensive chemotherapy.

I had officially started a new job as Headmaster of Cumnor House School only a few days before we received the news and I tried to keep working, driving for an hour and a half to Croydon each morning, working for the full day, and then driving home for another hour and a half in the evening. I tried to keep all the balls in the air, but I knew this was not sustainable. I wanted to be with Denise and to support her through her treatment.

Our lives became a frantic blur, an untethered blur. It felt to me as if we, as a family, had been hurled into middle of an angry, turbulent ocean and that, with wave after wave crashing around our heads, the best we could do was to keep our heads above water and somehow try to survive.

You need to look forward, to focus on the present challenge, and yet, at times such as this, it's hard not to look back. I couldn't help it. I was kicking myself because I kept wondering whether the situation could have been avoided.

Could we have caught the cancer earlier, before it had spread? Should we have caught the cancer earlier? Why had I not seen the signs, and done something? Why? The signs were there. They were clear. Why had I not insisted Denise go to the doctor? Why had I not insisted she have the tests?

Was I being irrational? Maybe. Was there any point in such thoughts? Maybe not, and yet all the signs had been there, hadn't they?

More than two months earlier, in the middle of June, Denise had said she was feeling tired. It's nothing, we had thought. It's normal for a teacher to feel exhausted in the last five or six weeks of the summer term, when there is so much to be done.

She had worked at the same school for 33 years, starting in 1983 when it was called Christ Church Junior School and continuing through an amalgamation with another school in 2011, after which it was renamed as Christ The Saviour Church of England Primary School, in Ealing. Her skill in leading the education of children with special needs for so many years ensured she was respected on all sides, and her remarkable warmth, empathy and kindness meant she was truly loved by colleagues and generations of pupils.

She said she felt tired, which was unusual for her, but we persuaded ourselves it was normal. There were other signs: she started to eat less, she declined the usual glass of Prosecco she enjoyed with her meal at the weekend, she cancelled sessions with her trainer because she said exercise was too painful. Was this normal? Well, it was normal for a teacher to be tired, wasn't it?

After the end of the summer term, at the start of the holidays, we travelled to Cornwall to attend the wedding of our niece Tamsin, daughter of Denise's sister Liz, in St Ives. It was a happy and beautiful day, and everything went well, but I saw Denise didn't drink at all, even for the toast. I asked her if she was OK. She assured me she felt fine but said she just didn't want any alcohol.

The following week, back home in Hanwell, she spent each day lying on the sofa, saying she felt lethargic. Right, enough is enough, I said, it was now time for us to see a doctor. Denise agreed. The first doctor asked if we thought she may be depressed. We said this seemed unlikely. The second doctor suggested she may have an iron deficiency, and prescribed tablets.

She still felt tired and washed-out. We were not getting anywhere.

"Come on," I said one morning. "Let's go on holiday. You've always wanted to take me to the Greek islands. Maybe you just need a break."

"OK, that sounds great," she said.

We booked a last-minute trip to a villa near the village of Lourdata, on the south coast of the island of Cephalonia. Ollie was busy at work, so Denise, Lewis, Josh and me made the trip. It should have been a wonderful week. The weather, the villa, the restaurants, the deep blue sea... everything was perfect, except Denise was not well. If anything, she became more tired. I wanted to be positive. I wanted to convince everybody, not least myself, that everything was going to be fine, but my wife's health was deteriorating before our eyes.

We arrived back in London and immediately arranged to see the doctor, who organised a series of tests. We will get the results next week, he said, certainly before the August Bank Holiday weekend.

"All right," I suggested, "we have got a few free days now. Why don't we drive down to Cornwall and see your family?"

"Really," she sighed. "It's such a long drive."

"Come on, Denise," I insisted. "Let's make the effort."

We drove to Penzance the next day, and arranged to have lunch with some of Denise's family at the Apple Tree Café in Sennen, owned by Stephen Clemens, the husband of our niece Amy. Everything went well, and we both enjoyed seeing everybody again, as usual, but her sisters were clearly concerned.

"Something is wrong," one of them said. "This is not the Denise we know."

I wanted to disagree. I wanted to say she was fine. I wanted to say that all she needed was a decent rest. I wanted to wish this away.

After a couple of days in Cornwall, we drove back to London and, in the blink of an eye, it was Friday 26 August, 2016, and we were sitting in the doctor's room, receiving the hammer blow.

The further tests followed and, within ten days, Denise was admitted to the Cromwell Hospital, in South Kensington, having a small disc inserted under the skin of her chest, which served as a port through which all the chemotherapy drugs could be more easily drip-dripped into her veins.

Treatment started in September, and continued into October. It was a gruelling schedule. Denise was admitted to the Cromwell every two weeks and, each time, she would stay in a private room for three days. The drugs were dripped into her veins very slowly, over a period of 48 hours.

Denise tolerated the treatment well at first but, as we moved into the third and fourth sessions, the cumulative effect of the drugs began to take its toll, and she would be wiped out for a couple of days afterwards.

We arranged to see the doctor again after the fourth treatment, and he seemed pleased with her progress. The liver functions were picking up, he said, which was a positive sign. I looked at Denise. She looked at me. We both seemed to be searching for confirmation from the other that this was indeed good news, that we had turned the corner, that this was a glimpse of light at the end of what seemed a long and dark tunnel.

I took Lewis and Josh back to their respective universities, something Denise and I had previously done together, and so enjoyed doing together. Ollie, our oldest, remained in London, where he was working. I continued to drive back and forth to Cumnor House School, determined to fulfil my responsibilities as headmaster and to care for Denise at the same time. My employers, Cognita, and indeed everybody at the school, could not have been more understanding and supportive in increasingly difficult circumstances.

It was just after half past three on the afternoon of Monday 10 October, 2016, and I was preparing to run a staff meeting at Cumnor House. My mobile phone rang. I saw Ollie's name appear on the screen, and answered.

"Yes, Ollie?"

"Dad, I have just been speaking to Mum on the phone," he said. "She started talking nonsense. She doesn't sound right at all."

"All right, son," I replied. "I will call the hospital now."

I managed to reach one of the doctors, and explained what had happened. He told me to get Denise to the Cromwell as soon as possible. I knew she was at home with Jen Moseley, one of her closest friends, so I phoned Jen and asked her to take Denise in a cab to the Cromwell. I said I was going to drive as fast as possible from Croydon and meet them there.

Denise suffered three major seizures during the hours that followed. It seemed as though the cancer had spread to her brain. At least, that is what one of the doctors indicated. As I waited with Ollie, who had arrived from work, in a private room nearby, we started to fear the worst. I phoned Lewis and Josh, and suggested they come home immediately.

Three times, we seemed to be losing her. Three times, the doctors and nurses managed to bring her back. Denise had been taken to the Intensive Care Unit but she rallied and recovered. In fact, at lunch time the following day, she was sitting up in her bed, quiet but calm, with our three sons and me sitting around her.

What now, I wondered. One doctor said a course of radiotherapy, focused on the membrane around the brain, would bring things back under control, while another doctor suggested we should focus on containing rather than curing the disease. I was listening intently, trying to understand what was happening, desperately trying to interpret every nuance in what was being said, bouncing between hope and reality. At times, it felt as though I was learning an entirely new language, the complex language of cancer care.

Denise's condition remained stable for a few weeks, and she received a steady stream of visits from her brothers and sisters. Some days she appeared fine and in good spirits. Other days were a little bit harder.

"Floyd, please promise me something," she said one afternoon.

"Of course," I said. "What is it?"

"If things get really bad, I don't want the boys to see me suffering. Promise me you will not let them see me like that."

"OK, I understand."

She suffered another serious setback in the first week of November, apparently caused by some kind of lung infection. The doctors were concerned and, once again, I felt it was necessary to call Lewis and Josh back from university. Once again, Denise somehow summoned the strength to recover, and to perk up and, again, for a few days, it felt as though hope was gaining the upper hand in what had become an ongoing struggle with reality.

The two younger boys returned to their studies, and I asked Ollie to go back to work and get on with things. He didn't want to go. I said we need to carry on with our lives as much as possible, even if, in fact, I had decided it was time for me to step away from Cumnor House School, to stop trying to keep going on all fronts and to spend all my time with Denise.

So many people stepped forward. Jen Moseley and Debbie Chetwyn, two great friends in London, stayed close, and her quartet of younger sisters – Sally, Sue, Mandy and Janet – regularly visited, and helped. Jan and John Kirman continued to support me and the boys. Denise would come home for a few days, and then return to hospital, and then come home again; all the while, we wrapped her in love, empathy and kindness.

"Dad, we're not going to lose Mum, are we?" Josh asked.

"Son, I just don't know," I replied. "It's possible. I am sorry."

In these most difficult moments, I felt it was important to be honest. It would have been much easier to say 'no, don't worry, everything is going to be fine', and quickly to change the subject and move on to something else, but that would not have been fair on him. He deserved to know what was happening, so he could deal with the reality, however difficult it may be.

Denise's condition deteriorated again on Wednesday 16 November. She was on a drip, and she seemed to have no energy at all. A physiotherapist implored her to do some gentle exercises in bed, but she was barely able to sit up, and she gently slipped into what became a deep coma.

I asked a doctor bluntly: "How long does she have left?"

"I'm sorry," he said, "but probably no later than Monday."

First, I contacted each of the boys, explained what had happened and let them know that, this time, it was possible Denise was not going to recover. I phoned her sister Sue and updated her, and she helpfully relayed the news to the rest of the Friggens family. Jen Moseley and Debbie Chetwyn came to visit again, effectively to say a final goodbye to their friend.

Each hour passed slowly and, by Sunday morning, the three boys and I were sitting around her bed, trying to take in what was happening, trying to support each other. I remembered my promise.

"Listen," I said. "Your mother did not want you to see her like this. Go home, get something to eat and rest. I will let you know if anything happens, but you don't need to be here."

Lewis and Josh went home, but Ollie insisted on remaining at the hospital, and found somewhere to rest. Throughout this ordeal, my oldest son had been a tower of strength. I was so proud of him.

Denise, my wife, died at the Cromwell Hospital at three minutes before nine o'clock on the evening of Sunday 20 November, 2016.

The formalities followed and, when the paperwork was complete, Jen came to collect me. I was carrying Denise's belongings in a bag, and we arrived home in the early hours of the morning. The boys were still up. We talked, and we remembered, and we cried. We were utterly bereft.

I remember waking up on the Monday morning, and feeling alone, completely alone for the first time in almost four decades. Denise had gone. The sense of finality was brutal. Her absence was intolerable. In such circumstances, in the midst of trauma, a kind of auto-pilot seems to kick in.

First, I headed to the Register Office, where I applied for the death certificate. Then I drove to Christ The Saviour School in Ealing, where Denise had taught and been so happy for so long, and I explained exactly what had happened to Raymond Prentice, the Executive Head, and to Katie Tramoni, the Head of School, and to other senior colleagues who had known Denise so well.

I committed myself to making the necessary arrangements, partly because I wanted to be meticulous and to get everything correct, but also because I felt a strong urge to keep myself busy.

The funeral was held at Christ the Saviour at 14:00 on Friday 9 December. More than 450 family and friends filled the school's church, and another 300 people gathered to watch a live video stream of the service, including approximately 200 in the Great Hall, and another 100 in the Church Hall.

A total of 750 people came to pay their respects to Denise, in what was a truly extraordinary turn-out, and everyone seemed to appreciate the readings, the music and the eulogies. I spoke. One of her former pupils spoke. Her sister Susan spoke. Her friend Jen spoke. Raymond Prentice spoke. The school could not have been more supportive, providing food and drink for everyone afterwards in the Great Hall.

Only close relatives attended a private cremation at Mortlake Crematorium in Barnes at 16:00, but everybody was then invited to gather in the clubhouse of the Ealing Trailfinders rugby club from 16:30 onwards. Denise and I were both members and the boys had all played in the junior section. Once again, the club, and specifically the club president, Dick Craig, a good friend of mine, could not have been more kind and generous.

Mourners were invited to wear something vibrant, and I had decided to wear my yellow and black Cornwall county rugby scarf. Everybody was extremely kind to me and the boys, and, by the time we got home, we were relieved and pleased to have hosted what was a fitting tribute, which brought together all the different strands of Denise's remarkable life.

We had honoured... Denise, the proud daughter and sister from west Cornwall... Denise the long-serving, dedicated teacher... Denise the loyal friend... and, Denise the loving mother and the wonderful, compassionate, supportive and most perfect wife.

With Christmas approaching, my three sons and I started what was inevitably going to be a long and difficult process, as we tried to move forward and cope with the reality of being bereaved.

# Chapter 12

# **Revived**

Denise left me with many blessings... with almost 40 years of happy memories, and with three extraordinary sons. We had raised them together, and the task of providing them with love and support now fell to me, alone.

Ollie, Lewis and Josh have grown into impressive people, distinct individuals, but they are also a tight and formidable team.

Oliver James Steadman is our oldest, born on February 3, 1993. I very nearly missed his birth. Denise was in the maternity unit of the Ealing Hospital and, late at night, nothing was happening. You may as well go home, she told me. We lived five minutes away, so I went back and slept.

"Floyd, Floyd, wake up!"

"Floyd, you have to wake up!"

It was the early hours of the morning, and our neighbour, Wanda Hingle, was throwing stones at our bedroom window, screaming and shouting.

I looked out the window, wondering what on earth was happening.

"Denise has gone into labour! You must go to the hospital now! Hurry up!"

I pulled on my clothes, drove back to the hospital and arrived in the maternity unit barely five minutes before our son was born. It was an incredible moment of pure and undiluted happiness. I know it was not a unique event. More than 140 million babies are born in the world each and every year. It was, however, unique for us, and we were overwhelmed with joy.

Ollie has always seemed serious and intelligent, a thinker. Like his mother, he knows his own mind. In 2000, when he was seven, we had planned for him to go to school at Colet Court, where I was employed as a senior teacher, which meant we qualified for a substantial reduction in fees. It was a fine school.

"No," said our seven-year-old son, unequivocally. "I don't want to go there. I won't know anyone there. I want to go to school with my friends. I want to go to Hobbayne Primary School, here in Hanwell."

"But, Ollie..."

"No, Dad, please understand me. I want to go to Hobbayne."

All right, I said. I won't pretend I was delighted. Nothing was more important than education, and my son was turning down an opportunity to attend one of the best independent prep schools in London, which would help him get excellent grades because he was so bright, and that would help him get into a leading university, where he would get a top class degree, and then a great job... and now, aged seven, he was ready to sacrifice all this because he wanted to go to school with his mates at the local primary.

What would happen if he fell in with the wrong crowd, and never realised his potential? We had worked so hard to give him the opportunities we had never had, and now...

Denise listened patiently, and then said we must support him. She was right, of course. I relented and said, OK, Hobbayne could be Plan A but, if that didn't work out, we could switch to Colet Court as Plan B.

Ollie made it work, brilliantly, and has never looked back. He excelled in class and in sport, moved on to Drayton Manor High School, continued to achieve and was eventually invited to apply to attend Oxford University.

"No, Dad," he said. "I'm not going to Oxford."

"All right," I said, "where do you want to go?"

"I want to stay in London, and go to Kings or Imperial or UCL."

"That's fine, but what's your back-up plan?"

"I don't need a back-up plan, Dad. I'll make it work in London."

He did make it work, eventually securing an honours degree in neuroscience at King's College, London, and he has since embarked upon a successful working career, making the most of his intelligence, his creativity and his determination, to a point where he has become the co-founder of a tech company.

Ollie blazed the trail, and his younger brothers were eager to follow, going to school at Hobbayne Primary, and then at Drayton Manor.

Lewis Alexander Steadman is our second son, born on February 25, 1996. The experts say parents are often more relaxed in raising their second children, when everything seems less new and frightening, with the result that many second children turn out to be relaxed and easygoing. By nature, Lewis would seem to suggest this particular theory is proven.

He also thrived at primary and high school, and became not only Deputy Head Boy but also captain of the rugby first XV at Drayton Manor. He demonstrated an ability to enthuse and engage people, to lead.

All the boys played rugby both at school and in the excellent junior section of our local club, Ealing Trailfinders RFC, but they also played cricket, tennis and football as well. Sport has always been something we enjoyed as a family, although we have generally preferred to play rather than to watch.

Lewis and his friends were particularly eager to drive standards in the rugby at Drayton Manor, and the team certainly got stronger during their time, winning more and more matches on the London circuit.

"I want to study mathematics at university," Lewis declared one day.

"Really? Are you sure?" Denise and I asked, almost in unison.

"Yes," he replied, smiling. "I really enjoy maths. I want to do maths."

He secured a place to study at The University of Manchester, from where he emerged with an honours degree in maths. He proceeded to find a job working in software development at a financial services company, and has since joined Apple Inc, the multinational technology leader... and has continued to prosper, smiling, popular and cheerful.

Joshua Charles Steadman is our third son, born on September 30, 1997; we soon realised that Josh, as we called him, had inherited from his father a relatively short and stocky build.

This physique served me well on the rugby field and, as he made his way along the well-trodden path through Hobbayne and Drayton Manor, Josh emerged as a talented, strong and effective full back or outside centre. He played in the Middlesex County team, and he took great pleasure in earning selection ahead of rivals from more prestigious independent schools.

I was enormously proud of his achievements, not least because I knew exactly how he felt. When I was his age, as a pupil at Kingsbury High School, I had been hugely frustrated when I was left out of the

Middlesex side because the county selectors preferred a player from Harrow School. Forty years later, it was good to see my youngest son getting a fair crack of the whip.

His performances started to attract attention from major independent schools eager to recruit talented players, and we received approaches from Hampton School, St Benedict's School and Harrow School, who wanted Josh to join them for his last two years at school, to study his A levels and play rugby. I was open-minded. Rugby teams at such schools typically trained two or three times a week in fantastic facilities; the Drayton Manor side was training once a week on a decent playing field. It would surely make sense to...

"Dad, I don't want to move anywhere," Josh said emphatically. "I want to stay at Drayton Manor, and stay with my friends."

So he stayed, and performed extremely well, and eventually advanced to the University of Southampton, from where he emerged with an honours degree in biochemistry. He continued to enjoy his rugby, playing for the London Irish Wild Geese team, the amateur team of the famous Exiles in south-west London. He now works as a Junior Software Integration Engineer.

Our three sons have always been close and supportive of each other. I'm sure this has helped each of them get through what has been a challenging period in their lives, as they have come to terms with the loss of their mother. I have also tried to support them, and they have been a huge source of support for me.

Since I have taken this opportunity to set down some thoughts about them, it seems only fair to let them have their say as well...

Ollie reflects: "The saying 'life's not fair' has been mentioned more than a few times in our home... Dad can be quite rigid and he always wants to stick to the rules... he seems engaged in a constant battle to prove himself... he has always chosen passive resistance, and is not consumed by injustice... he has taught in independent schools, rather than state schools, and become a role model... I have met students who genuinely seem to love him... my mother's family have welcomed him with open arms, and they mean a lot to him."

Lewis reflects: "Dad has always been an inspirational figure in our lives... we joke about him always sitting on the fence and always being scrupulously fair in everything he says and does... he used to force us to split the tips from our newspaper round 50/50, even though I worked much longer... he has always been spurred on to prove people wrong, and he will always stand up for the underdog, whether it's a black rugby player who is not getting a fair chance in a team or a student who is struggling at school."

Josh reflects: "Dad has been popular wherever he works... I recall somebody saying he was a brilliant headmaster because he always made a special point of standing on the steps at the main entrance of the school at the start and at the end of every single day, saying good morning to everyone as they arrived and saying goodbye to everyone as they left for home... his mental strength is amazing, especially when our mother was unwell... he says he will retire, but it's hard to believe he will ever stop working."

There... they have had their say. That's enough. I remain hugely proud of each of them, and I love being their father. I love catching up with them, love hearing their news, love driving them to where they need to be, love taking them for a meal, love meeting their friends, and these days, maybe above all, love seeing the way they act and speak, recognising traits inherited from their mother.

We have each other, and we still have Denise's large family in Cornwall, always checking up on us, always keeping an eye on us.

Our three boys have no fewer than 21 cousins, from the Friggens line, children of Denise's three brothers and seven sisters. Randal had two, Neville and Lisa. John had two sons, Stephen and Andrew. Angela had two, a daughter named Nicky and a son named Jamie. Liz had the same, Tamsin and James. Jeff had two girls, Sophie and Lucy. Sue had four, two girls called Amy and Kate, who is my god daughter, and two boys named Tom and Joe.

That's 14 and counting. Sally had three, Ryan, Megan and Murray. Mandy had two, Charlotte and Naomi. And Denise's sister Janet had two children, Luke and Jess. That's a grand total of 21.

I apologise if these paragraphs read like the opening section of Numbers, in the Old Testament, where Elizur was the son of Shedeur, who was the son of Simeon etc. but our Cornish relatives have always played, and continue to play an important role in our lives. We feel like we belong.

After Denise died, I returned to work as headmaster at Cumnor House School in Croydon but, after two terms, the combination of the long commute and the work proved too demanding. I will always be grateful to Simon Camby, then the Group Director of Education at Cognita, for his pragmatism and understanding during what was a challenging time.

Simon and I eventually agreed I would return to Clifton Lodge Prep School, one of my former schools, as Executive Head, working part-time, for three days in each week. This was an ideal solution since it enabled me to continue the work we had started, and also to support my sons.

With the support of a considerate employer and a host of wonderful friends, I was able to cope and to start to build a new life without Denise. I was grieving, and adapting, and slowly seeking a new way forward.

On May 25, 2020, not far from the intersection of East 38th Street and Chicago Avenue in the Powderhorn Park suburb of Minneapolis, Minnesota in the United States of America, a police officer named Derek Chauvin attempted to restrain a black man arrested on suspicion of using a counterfeit $20 note. In doing so, he knelt on the man's neck for more than nine minutes.

The black man died, handcuffed and lying face-down on the street. His name was George Floyd, and the appalling manner of his death sparked worldwide demonstrations against police brutality and racism. Around 20 million people participated in 'Black Lives Matter' protests in the US.

It appeared to be a tipping point. People had had enough. General awareness of racial prejudice quickly rose to once unimagined levels all around the world, and people more swiftly and more strongly objected against any form of racial discrimination in any area of life. For their part, sportsmen and women started to show solidarity by 'taking the knee' before kick-off.

I watched all these events unfold with great interest, and was encouraged by what appeared to be a genuine shift in public opinion. For so much of my life, racial discrimination had been effectively tolerated, and almost regarded as a joke. Now, at last, it was being universally condemned.

Players opting to 'take the knee', most notably before Premier League football matches, and sporadically before Premiership rugby matches, has sometimes been controversial. Some have dug into the past of the BLM campaign, which actually started in 2013, and suggested the players are unwittingly supporting a movement which is fundamentally anti-Semitic. Such people are missing the point. The 'taking of the knee' is a gesture by young sports people, who want to make a stand against racial abuse... that's all.

My main concern was that such a gesture, in fact any gesture, will ultimately be insufficient unless it is backed by actions, and the action needed to address racial abuse is education.

Such discrimination is almost always the direct result of fear and ignorance. Effective education counters both.

I admired the decision of the England football team to take the knee before all of their matches during the UEFA European Championships, played in 2021. They were heavily criticised in some quarters, not least by some members of the Government, but manager Gareth Southgate, captain Harry Kane and others stuck to their principles, refused to be bullied and effectively conveyed a clear and simple message that racial abuse and discrimination will not be tolerated, either by spectators in the stadium or online on social media platforms.

In the eyes of millions around the world, they courageously and effectively ensured the message was kept alive.

When Southgate calls out the racists, it makes a difference. When Kane says it is simply not acceptable, it makes a difference. When talented young black men like Raheem Sterling and Marcus Rashford are prepared to address issues beyond the game, and conduct themselves with bravery, integrity, intelligence and empathy, it most certainly makes a difference.

Many maintain the large social media companies have an important role to play in eradicating racist comments from their platforms. I have heard people suggest identification documents should be required to open an account on Twitter or Instagram in exactly the same way that they are required to open a bank account. In this way, people who post racist comments, or other forms of hate, could be quickly identified and efficiently punished.

I am not so sure. In far too many places around the world, social media has provided a precious platform for persecuted people to speak out against cruel oppression and tyranny, and to do so anonymously without fear of retribution by the authorities. Are we certain we want to insist on ID with accounts, and effectively remove the right of free speech for such people?

The issue is alive and current but, to repeat, I believe it will only be resolved by sustained education over an extended period of time.

Who bears responsibility for education? We all do. Teachers in schools should feel able and empowered to address racism in and out of the classroom. The media, in all its forms, has a significant role to play, consistently to stress that nobody should ever be judged by the colour of their skin. Public figures, even 'celebrities', can influence the way people behave, if they are prepared to raise their voices and speak out against racism in all its forms. And, perhaps most importantly, parents have a critical role to reinforce the message.

In these ways, a society, even a global society, can be educated and changed, and fear and ignorance can be confronted and reduced.

I am optimistic about the future of race relations, both in the United Kingdom and around the world. Many issues remain, of course, and I am certainly not minimising the work that needs to be done. However, we should not lose sight of the fact that society has come a long way in the past 20, 30, 40 years, and the momentum is certainly moving in the right direction.

In my time, when I was at school and playing rugby, casual racism was widely tolerated and we, as the targets, were left with no option but to accept the insults, keep our heads down and move on. It's not an exaggeration to say any player's rugby career would have been seriously affected if they had decided to speak out against racism during the 1980s. They would have been targeted by certain elements of the media, and branded as a troublemaker. The fact this is no longer the case is certainly a reason to celebrate.

This may sound like a sweeping statement but, in general, younger people are more inclined to expose and oppose racism than their parents were. The future belongs to them, so the future is brighter than our past.

One example is the experience of my own family. Within four generations, we have progressed from my grandparents, who were poor labourers working on the land in Jamaica with no money and apparently no hope, to my sons, who are bright and bold, thriving in every way. In so many ways, the progress of this branch of the Steadman family has been truly staggering.

There's no doubt. The momentum is moving in the right direction.

Against this background, I have taken a pro-active interest in matters relating to diversity and inclusion, supporting various organisations in this area, and I have started speaking more regularly, generally in schools, often to members of staff, on the challenge of addressing unconscious bias. Once again, the most effective solution is education, education, education.

I retired as the part-time Executive Head at Clifton Lodge Preparatory School at Easter 2020 and spent most of the pandemic in west London. In the summer of 2021, I moved to base myself in west Cornwall to be closer to... I almost said Denise's family... now I can say 'my family'.

A property had become available in the parish of Ludgvan, adjacent to Crowlas and near Penzance. It is a beautiful part of the world, a place where I feel completely at home, surrounded by friends and family, so I decided to take the plunge, to renovate this house with spectacular views to the east, and to start a new way of life.

It is sometimes said that retirement is fine, so long as you have a good job to go to, and I suppose I may be the living proof. In truth, I have only retired from full-time employment and created the time and space for me to make a meaningful contribution to several projects and causes that enthuse me.

Among the roles and responsibilities that keep me regularly bouncing back and forth between west Cornwall and west London, I continue to serve on the governing body of two outstanding independent schools, Hampton School and St Augustine's Priory, a girls school in Ealing.

I am also an active supporter of the Drive Forward Foundation, a charity supporting people aged between 16 and 26 as they strive to transition from a life in care into a career.

Every now and then, I will make contact with my good friends John Buckton and Steve Ravenscroft, another notable Saracens player and administrator, and the three of us make arrangements to meet up and go to watch a rugby match, usually involving either Saracens or England.

First and last, I suppose, I am the product of my experiences. After everything that has happened over the past 63 years, through all the challenges, through all the happy days and the sad days, I have worked hard to be nothing more and nothing less than a decent man doing his best.

At times I have been content to have survived but now, looking forward to what lies ahead, I am starting to feel revived.

# Photograph credits

Most of the photographs in this book have been provided by the Steadman family, with the following exceptions:

**Section 1**
Pages 4 and 5
Dive pass vs Ealing *(© Peter Jenkins, From the back of a Motorbike)*

**Section 2**
Page 2
Celebrating with supporters *(© Colorsport)*
Clearing against Wasps *(© Colorsport)*

Page 3
With Jason Leonard *(© Peter Jenkins, From the back of a Motorbike)*
Tackling Wasps hooker *(© Peter Jenkins, From the back of a Motorbike)*

# Index